NATIONAL AUDUBON SOCIETY

FIRST
FIELD
GUIDE

BIRDS

Scholastic Inc.

New York Toronto London Auckland Sydney

NATIONAL AUDUBON SOCIETY

FIRST FIELD GUIDE

BIRDS

The National Audubon Society, established in 1905, has 550,000 members and more than 500 chapters nationwide. Its mission is to conserve and restore natural ecosystems, focusing on birds and other wildlife, and these guides are part of that mission. Celebrating the beauty and wonders of nature, Audubon looks toward its second century of educating people of all ages. For information about Audubon membership, contact:

National Audubon Society

700 Broadway

New York, NY 10003-9562

212-979-3000   800-274-4201

http://www.audubon.org

LIBRARY OF CONGRESS CATALOGING-IN-PUBLICATION DATA
Weidensaul, Scott.
National Audubon Society first field guide to birds/Scott Weidensaul.
p. cm.
Includes index.
Summary: An informative, visual guide to the natural science of birds as well as a field guide to over 150 species found in North America.
ISBN 0-590-05482-1   ISBN 0-590-05446-5
1. Birds—Juvenile literature. 2. Birds—North America—Juvenile literature.
[1. Birds.]   I. National Audubon Society.
II. Title.
QL676.2.W455   1998
598'.097—dc21   97-17989   CIP   AC

ISBN 0-590-05446-5 (HC)
ISBN 0-590-05482-1 (PB)

10 9 8 7 6 5 4 3 2 1   8   9/9   0/0   01   02

Printed in Hong Kong
First printing, April 1998

Contents

About this book

Whether you are watching birds in your own backyard, taking a vacation at the shore, or hiking in the mountains, this book will help you look at birds the way a naturalist does. The book is divided into four parts:

Northern Cardinal page 132

PART 1: The world of birds

tells you how birds are named, what makes them so perfectly suited to life in the air, how they migrate, where they lay their eggs, and how they raise their young.

PART 2: How to look at birds

gives you the information you need to begin identifying birds; provides fascinating facts about birds' colors, shapes, bills, and songs; explains the difference between a bird's range and its habitat; and describes the plights of several endangered species.

PART 3: The field guide

includes detailed descriptions, range maps, and dramatic photographs of 50 common North American birds. In addition, this section provides helpful shorter descriptions accompanied by photographs of 125 other important species.

PART 4: The reference section

at the back of the book includes an illustrated list of the 50 state birds; a helpful glossary of technical terms used by ornithologists; lists of useful books, videos, CDs, Web sites, and organizations; and an index of species covered in the Field Guide.

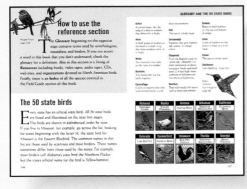

A spotter's guide:

This handy, pocket-sized card of 50 common North American birds will slip easily into your back pocket whenever you take a walk or a hike.

What is a naturalist?

A naturalist is an explorer of nature—someone curious about the natural world and how all its parts work together. Most naturalists are ordinary people, but some are scientists (such as ornithologists, who study birds). You can be a naturalist, too. All you need to do is to go outside and observe nature yourself.

John James Audubon

Florida Scrub Jays by John James Audubon

SOLDIER NATURALISTS

In the 1800s on the western frontier, many Army officers were naturalists—often despite great danger. In 1872 one military naturalist barely escaped the Apaches with the egg of a rare hawk hidden in his mouth!

Margaret Morse Nice

SELF-TAUGHT NATURALISTS

Perhaps the most famous naturalist to study birds was John James Audubon, who was born in Haiti and came to the United States in 1803 as a young man. Audubon was a self-taught artist who was fascinated by nature. He spent most of his life discovering and painting many new species of birds and mammals. Another respected naturalist was Margaret Morse Nice, an early American ornithologist who studied the Song Sparrows living near her home in Columbus, Ohio. Nice became one of the founders of behavioral science and was the first woman president of any ornithological society. She died in 1974.

Song Sparrow page 134

8

Essential equipment

The most important thing to take with you when you go birding is a good pair of binoculars. Take a small notebook and pencil, too, to record your observations. Many important discoveries have been made by amateur naturalists. You will also need a field guide, like this one, to help you identify species. Identification is the first step toward understanding the natural world.

A naturalist's code of ethics

- Be respectful of the natural world. In a sense you are a visitor in the home of others—the birds, mammals, and other animals living there.
- Be quiet and careful. Good observers have no effect on what they watch.
- Don't disturb nesting birds or collect birds' feathers, eggs, or nests. Leave baby birds alone.
- Learn about the environment and how to live in harmony with nature.

The world of birds

There are more than 9,000 bird species in the world, and scientists are still finding new ones. About 650 species of birds nest in North America; another 150 pass through each year. Our birds are amazingly varied in their sizes, shapes, colors, and behavior patterns.

Arctic Tern

Peregrine Falcon page 83

AVIAN SPEEDSTERS

The fastest animals on earth, Peregrine Falcons, may dive for prey at over 200 miles per hour.

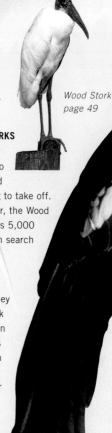

Wood Stork page 49

HOMEBODIES AND WANDERERS

Some birds are stay-at-homes, like the Downy Woodpecker, which rarely travels more than a few miles from its birthplace. The Arctic Tern, on the other hand, commutes from Alaska and northern Canada to Antarctica twice each year, a trip of more than 22,000 miles!

STREAMLINED SWALLOWS TO BULKY STORKS

Some birds, like the Tree Swallow, are sleek and streamlined, perfectly suited to flight. Others, such as the spindly-legged Wood Stork, appear too tall and gangling to take off. Despite its awkward appearance, however, the Wood Stork is an expert flier, soaring as high as 5,000 feet and flying up to 80 miles nonstop in search of the shallow pools in which it feeds.

EATING LIKE A BIRD

Some birds devour most anything that they happen upon; others are finicky and stick to just a few foods. The Common Grackle, for example, consumes seeds, insects, worms, frogs, even birds' eggs. The Cedar Waxwing, on the other hand, eats mostly fruit.

Cedar Waxwing page 133

GLIDERS, SPRINTERS, AND DIVERS

*Common Loon
page 50*

The hunting behavior of birds varies as much as their sizes and shapes. Turkey Vultures spend most of their time aloft, searching for dead animals on the ground. Roadrunners hunt on foot for desert insects and lizards, seldom taking to the air. Loons walk awkwardly and find most of their food by diving in the sea or in northern ponds.

FROM TINY HUMMERS TO MASSIVE VULTURES

Our native birds range in size from the tiny three-inch Calliope Hummingbird, which weighs less than a nickel and sips nectar, to the giant California Condor, a vulture that has a nine-foot wingspan and feeds only on dead animals.

California Condor

Calliope Hummingbird

11

What's in a name?

Dark-eyed Junco
page 135

The study of how living things are classified is called taxonomy. Every plant or animal belongs to several groups. The largest group is the kingdom. The animal kingdom includes any and all animals. This kingdom is separated into phyla. Each phylum breaks down into classes. The class Aves, which includes all birds, has 29 orders. Each order is broken down into families. Every family is divided into genera, which are subdivided into species.

Juncos from several parts of North America look very different, but they mate with each other so they are lumped together as one species, the Dark-eyed Junco.

LATIN SCIENTIFIC NAMES

Ornithologists give each bird a Latin scientific name, so people around the world will recognize it. A scientific name has two parts, the capitalized genus name and the species name. *Anas platyrhynchos*, the Mallard, and *Anas rubripes*, the American Black Duck, both belong to the same genus. The Wood Duck, *Aix sponsa*, does not.

12

Ame
page

TWO BIRD SPECIES CLASSIFIED

A Great Blue Heron and an Orchard Oriole both belong to the animal kingdom, of course. They also belong to the same phylum—Chordata—and to the same class—Aves—which means "birds" in Latin. Here the similarity ends, however. Each bird belongs to a different family, genus, and species.

Kingdom: Animalia
Phylum: Chordata
Class: Aves
Order: Ciconiiformes (herons, storks, flamingos)
Family: Ardeidae (all herons)
Genus: *Ardea* (large herons)
Species: *herodias* (Great Blue Heron)

Kingdom: Animalia
Phylum: Chordata
Class: Aves
Order: Passeriformes (all perching birds)
Family: Icteridae (meadowlarks and blackbirds)
Genus: *Icterus* (all orioles)
Species: *spurius* (Orchard Oriole)

FROM MANY ENGLISH NAMES TO ONE

The same birds used to have different names in different places. To end confusion, scientists gave each species a single English name. Now, a falcon, once called a windhover in one area and a killy-hawk in another, is known only as the American Kestrel.

WHAT'S A SPECIES?

Birds that breed with each other, but not with other birds, are considered to be one species. Species members look like each other and usually look different from other species. However, Alder Flycatchers and Willow Flycatchers look alike but are considered separate species because they don't breed with each other.

To classify birds, scientists study not only their appearances but also internal organs and behavior. Scientists also classify birds on the basis of DNA, tiny strands of genes in their cells. This has led to some surprising discoveries—for instance, some vultures may really be short-legged storks!

Black Vulture

rel

Avian anatomy

Equipped with feathers (nature's lightest and most effective insulating material), keen eyesight, and incredibly efficient hearts, birds are superbly built for flying. Their real secret, however, is in their

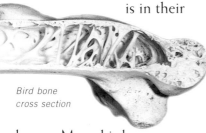

Bird bone cross section

bones. Many bird bones are hollow, saving weight, yet they have dozens of braces to strengthen them.

SKULL
The thin, light brain case has large eye sockets. The bill contains no teeth, thus reducing weight.

NECK
The neck is very flexible. Birds have up to seven more neck bones, or vertebrae, than humans.

WISHBONE
The wishbone, or clavicles, braces the wings. If its clavicles break, a bird can't fly.

Pigeon skeleton

BREASTBONE
The large breastbone, or sternum, protects the chest and belly and provides space for the attachment of wing muscles.

BIRDS' HEARTS BEAT FAST
Your pulse is usually about 70 to 90 beats per minute, but a Black-capped Chickadee's pounds away 500 times a minute. A hummingbird's heart may race at 1,260 beats a minute during the day, but drop to just 36 at night, when it slips into a deep sleep. *Black-capped Chickadee page 114*

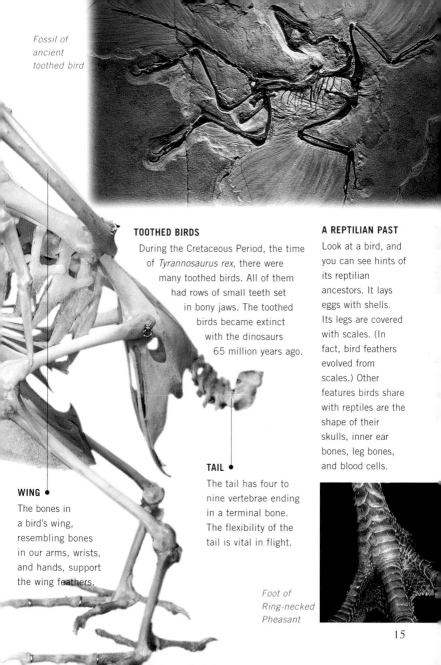

Fossil of ancient toothed bird

TOOTHED BIRDS

During the Cretaceous Period, the time of *Tyrannosaurus rex*, there were many toothed birds. All of them had rows of small teeth set in bony jaws. The toothed birds became extinct with the dinosaurs 65 million years ago.

A REPTILIAN PAST

Look at a bird, and you can see hints of its reptilian ancestors. It lays eggs with shells. Its legs are covered with scales. (In fact, bird feathers evolved from scales.) Other features birds share with reptiles are the shape of their skulls, inner ear bones, leg bones, and blood cells.

TAIL

The tail has four to nine vertebrae ending in a terminal bone. The flexibility of the tail is vital in flight.

WING

The bones in a bird's wing, resembling bones in our arms, wrists, and hands, support the wing feathers.

Foot of Ring-necked Pheasant

What makes a bird a bird? Feathers!

irds are the only creatures with feathers. "Light as a feather" is no exaggeration. Feathers weigh very little, but birds could not live without them. Feathers allow flight, provide terrific insulation, and keep rain and snow away from the skin. They can be colorful as a rainbow or make a bird blend in perfectly with its surroundings.

Mountain Bluebird preening, page 121

VANE

Feather barb

A FEATHER CLOSE-UP

You need a microscope to see that each barb in a feather's vanes is covered with tiny hooks that grip each other like miniature zippers. You can pull the barbs apart, then stroke them back together again with your fingertips. A bird does this with its beak when it preens.

SHAFT

The shaft is the long stiff quill that runs up the middle of every feather.

Contour feather

DOWN FEATHER

Soft and fluffy, down feathers grow under the body feathers and provide insulation.

CONTOUR FEATHER

A contour feather may be a large, stiff feather on the wing or tail like this one, or a smaller body feather. Every feather on a bird's body is controlled by a set of tiny muscles, which allows the bird to raise or lower them—fluffing its feathers on a cold day, for example.

AN INCREDIBLE QUANTITY OF FEATHERS

All the feathers on a bird's body are called its plumage. A tiny Ruby-throated Hummingbird has about 1,000 feathers; a White-throated Sparrow has about 2,000. A scientist once counted every feather on a Tundra Swan, from the largest wing quills to the tiniest fluff of down, and came up with 25,216.

VANE

The vanes on both sides of the shaft are made up of thousands of tiny strands called barbs.

Out with the old

Most birds replace their feathers every year, a few at a time, in a process called molting. A new feather grows out of the skin, inside a covering that looks like a straw; when it is fully grown, the cover peels away. Ducks and geese lose all their big wing feathers at once, so they are flightless for a few weeks in summer while the new ones grow in.

Tundra Swan page 57

How does a bird fly?

FLIGHT SCHOOL
A baby bird leaving the nest knows instinctively how to flap its wings. But it takes time for a young bird to become good at flying—time to practice and time for muscles to strengthen.

Just like an airplane's wing, a bird's wing is curved from front to back in a shape scientists call an airfoil. As the bird's wing flaps, air flows faster over the upward-curved top than it does across the bottom. Fast-moving air has less pressure than slow-moving air, so there is more pressure pushing up on the wing than there is pushing down, creating what scientists call lift. Lift is what gets a bird (or an airplane) into the air and helps keep it there.

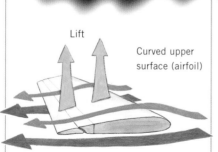

Airfoil

Lift

Curved upper surface (airfoil)

Airflow is slower over the lower surface, increasing upward pressure.

The fastest fliers

Most songbirds can fly about 20 to 30 miles per hour, but Common Eiders can fly nearly 50 miles per hour, and Dunlins (shorebirds) once caught up with and passed a plane flying 100 miles per hour. Peregrine Falcons are considered the fastest birds. Experts think they may reach 200 miles per hour in dives.

Female Mallard in gliding flight page 58

Four ways to fly

GLIDING

To glide, a bird stretches its wings out and sails along without flapping, dropping slowly toward the ground. Watch a goose or duck dropping down into a pond— that's a glide.

HOVERING

The best hoverers, hummingbirds, can stop in midair, flapping their wings over 50 times a second. Hummingbirds can also fly backward on purpose. No other birds can.

SOARING

Soaring is like gliding, but a bird finds warm, rising air to carry it upward. Hawks, eagles, and vultures are all excellent soarers; so are storks, cranes, and many other large birds.

FLAPPING

This is the most common kind of flight, but it uses a lot of energy. Most really fast birds use flapping flight.

19

How do birds migrate?

The seasonal trips made by birds are among the wonders of nature. Using nothing but muscles, feathers, and energy, birds of every size and shape travel thousands of miles.

Migrating waterfowl pass in front of the full moon.

FINDING THE WAY DURING THE DAY

Birds that fly by day use the sun along with the landscape to navigate. Hawks follow mountain ridges, and waterfowl stick close to major rivers.

FINDING THE WAY AT NIGHT

Scientists believe birds take advantage of natural clues to navigate. Those that fly at night use the position of the stars, just as oldtime sailors did. Birds also detect the invisible magnetic field that surrounds the earth—in fact, some species, like Bobolinks, have a tiny bit of a mineral called magnetite in their heads that may act as a compass.

CHAMPION MIGRATORS

Swainson's Hawks fly 7,000 miles from the western prairies to Argentina. Pacific Golden-Plovers fly more than 2,000 miles from Alaska to Hawaii—beating their wings twice a second for 35 hours without a rest. Many forest songbirds, such as warblers, vireos, and tanagers, migrate to the rain forests of Central and South America. Seabirds, like albatrosses and shearwaters, may fly entirely around the Pacific Ocean, not setting foot on land for almost a year.

Swainson's Hawk

WHY MIGRATE?

Birds migrate because they have to, not because they like to travel. Most migratory birds nest in the north, where it gets very cold in the winter. Cold weather itself isn't dangerous to birds (their feathers keep them insulated), but it makes it much harder to find foods such as insects, worms, frogs, or snakes. Lakes and ponds freeze in winter, forcing waterfowl, like ducks and geese, to migrate. But it isn't weather that tells a bird it's time to fly—it's the changing length of the day as spring or autumn approaches.

A Magnolia Warbler with an insect

NIGHT AND DAY

It's no surprise that owls migrate at night, but many songbirds that are usually active in daylight also migrate after dark—birds such as warblers, tanagers, thrushes, and vireos. They probably do this for a couple of reasons. They are protected from hawks, and flying at night leaves the daytime hours for feeding and resting. Plus, the nighttime air is cooler and damper, so they won't overheat as easily.

21

Where do birds lay their eggs?

Baltimore Oriole page 138

What a variety of nests birds make to hold their eggs and later their chicks! Orioles weave deep bags using strands of plant stems. Bald Eagles and Ospreys return to the same nests year after year, adding sticks, driftwood, and other debris until the piles weigh half a ton or more. Gulls, terns, and Killdeer just scrape away dirt, making shallow depressions.

HOW AMERICAN ROBINS MAKE THEIR NESTS

Adult robins first pick a forked tree branch or ledge. The male helps, but the female does most of the work, adding pieces of dead grass and mud to build a base, then laying down finer strands of grass to make the cup, and sitting in it every so often to make sure it fits her body.

*American Robin
page 122*

*Osprey
page 81*

BUILDING MATERIALS

Mud

Grass and twigs are common nest materials, but it's amazing what else gets into bird nests. Hummingbirds build nests from spiderwebs and lichens. Cliff Swallows use mud pellets to build vase-shaped nests. Ducks line their nests with down feathers plucked from their own breasts. Tufted Titmice add the paper-thin shed skins of snakes, and pieces of cellophane or plastic, which may look somewhat like snakeskins.

Snakeskin

Down feather

Grass

HELP BIRDS BUILD THEIR NESTS

A fun way to watch songbird behavior while helping those living in your area is to make nest material "donations" during the nesting season. Short lengths of cotton string or wool yarn are ideal for robins, orioles, and many others.

Where to build?

Not all birds nest in trees and bushes. Marsh Wrens and Red-winged Blackbirds weave nests among cattails. Grassland birds nest on the ground, and many birds use tree holes. Some holes are drilled by woodpeckers, which move to new ones the next year, leaving their holes for chickadees, nuthatches, and bluebirds—even kestrels and screech-owls.

A female Osprey incubates her eggs and waits for her mate to return with a fish for her dinner.

Bringing up chicks

The job of raising young birds begins with nest building. Once eggs are laid, the parents must keep them from getting cold, or the embryos inside will die. To make that job easier, incubating birds develop a brood patch—a featherless area on the breast that helps warm eggs with body heat.

Sandhill Crane chick page 47

A Yellow Warbler (page 131) feeding a Brown-headed Cowbird chick (page 141)

BABY-SITTERS

A few birds lay their eggs in other birds' nests and let them raise the babies. The most famous is the Brown-headed Cowbird, which lays its eggs in the nests of other songbirds, often tossing out the host's eggs first.

HELPING BABY BIRDS

Sometime you may find a baby bird that has just fledged and can't fly well. Leave it alone; it probably isn't abandoned even though you can't see its parents. They may be taking care of its brothers and sisters.

AFTER HATCHING

When songbird chicks hatch, they are naked, their eyes are closed, and they are able to do little more than hold up their wobbly heads and open their mouths. But young ducks and gamebirds, such as grouse and quail, are born covered in down and with their eyes open, able to feed almost immediately. A few hours after birth, baby Wood Ducks follow their mother out of the nest hole high in a tree—even though they can't fly! The babies fall to the ground, bounce a few times, and then waddle off after their mother, unharmed by the drop.

Parenting is hard work

Watch a nest of robins, House Finches, or other songbirds, and you'll quickly realize how hard the parents work. The chicks must be fed every few minutes, from sunup to sundown, until they are old enough to leave the nest, usually about two weeks after they hatch. Even after the young birds have left the nest, they must be fed and protected from predators. Gradually, they learn to live on their own.

Newly hatched songbird

Telling birds apart

How does a naturalist tell one bird from another at a glance? By looking for clues—called field marks—to the bird's identity. These are special markings, colors, or ways of behaving that set it apart from others.

Indigo Bunting
(male) page 121

Western Bluebird
(male)

Know how to look

When you see a bird you don't recognize, ask yourself these questions: Does this bird look as big as a robin or as small as a sparrow? Is it fat and round or long and skinny? (There's more about bird shapes on pages 30 and 31.) Then look at the color. If it is shiny dark blue all over and the size of a sparrow, it may be a male Indigo Bunting. But if it is larger, with an orangish breast and a blue back, it is a male bluebird—but which type? If it has a blue throat, it is a Western Bluebird. If its throat is orangish, it is an Eastern Bluebird. Look at the face and head because many field marks are found there, such as the crest of a Blue Jay or the black mask of a Cedar Waxwing.

Field marks

As you read through a field guide, you may come across unfamiliar words like "eye line" and "wing bar." These are terms that naturalists use to describe particular field marks. You can think of them as clues that will help you solve the mystery of which bird you're watching.

WING BARS •

Bars, either light or dark, that you can see near the front of the folded wings, like the white bars on this Yellow-rumped Warbler.

RUMP •

The feathers just in front of the top of the tail. Many birds have light rumps, such as the Northern Flicker.

26

EYE RING
A thin circle of color—usually black, sometimes red or white—around the bird's eye.

EYE LINE
Stripe above or across the bird's eye, like the black and white lines on a Red-eyed Vireo.

Red-eyed Vireo page 126

Northern Flicker page 101

Yellow-rumped Warbler page 128

FLASH MARKS
Markings seen only when the bird flies, like the white wing and tail markings of a mockingbird, or the yellow underwings of a Northern Flicker.

27

Why are birds different colors?

Colors help birds recognize their own kind, attract mates, and warn rivals. Usually the males of a species are more colorful than the females. A male American Goldfinch,

*American
Goldfinch
(male)
page 144*

for example, has a yellow body and black forehead and wings, but the female is duller, making her less conspicuous as she sits on their nest.

GROWING UP

As birds grow up, they molt their feathers several times, changing markings with each molt. Bald Eagles are brown when they leave the nest. It takes them five years to grow white head- and tail-feathers. Young robins have spotted breasts that don't turn orange until they get adult feathers late in summer.

28

Western Tanager (male)
page 139

Feather colors

Some colors you can see in a feather are caused by substances called pigments. Reds, oranges, and yellows come from pigments known as carotenoids. Melanins are pigments that give feathers their black, brownish, or gray colors. Melanins make a feather stronger, which is why white birds, such as gulls and terns, have black at their wing ends, protecting the feather tips from wear and tear. The white color of the plumage of birds such as ptarmigans and gulls, on the other hand, is caused by cells containing no pigments.

HIDING, SHOWING OFF

A bird's plumage can either help it blend in with its surroundings, like the speckled feathers of a Ruffed Grouse or Common Nighthawk, or make it more visible, like the bright colors of a male Baltimore Oriole or Western Tanager. Markings that help a bird hide (called camouflage) are a defense against predators. American Bitterns have stripes like the marsh reeds where they live, and ptarmigans, which live in the Arctic and in snow-covered mountains, grow white feathers in winter.

Immature Bald Eagles page 80

WHAT CAUSES IRIDESCENCE

The flashing red of a hummingbird's throat, or the deep blue of a Western Bluebird, are created by special cells in the feather barbs. These cells reflect only certain colors in sunlight back to your eyes, depending on the angle at which light hits them. That's why an Indigo Bunting can look blue one moment or almost black the next, if the bird moves slightly.

Ptarmigan (winter plumage)

Looking at shapes

American Kestrel
page 84

Bird-watchers can often identify birds that are very far away, or are silhouetted against the sky. They can't see the bird's field marks, so how do they know what it is? The answer lies in the bird's shape. For example, an American Kestrel and a Mourning Dove are about the same size, but their shapes are very different.

Mourning Dove page 90

A kestrel has a long, squared tail and a large head. The dove has a long, pointy tail and a small head.
Most birds fit into about a dozen basic body shapes (see page 44), and knowing them will help you narrow down the possibilities.

Belted Kingfisher page 111

Telling similar birds apart

The Belted Kingfisher and the Blue Jay have similar colors, both have crests, and they share the same overall shape of a perching bird, so you have to look closely to distinguish them. The Belted Kingfisher (above) is a plump, roundish bird with a very large bill; the Blue Jay (left) is slimmer with a much shorter bill and a smaller head.

Blue Jay
page 110

*Green Heron
page 47*

Shapes change

Legs and beaks make a big
difference in a bird's shape. A Green Heron and a small duck are about
the same size, but the heron's long legs, neck, and bill give it a much different
shape. Remember that a bird's shape can change. You may be fooled at first
by a heron sitting with its neck folded tightly against its body.
Also, on a cold day, a bird will fluff its feathers, making itself
look fatter and rounder than on a warm day.

Good posture!

Watch a robin—when it runs or hops it holds its
head low, but when it stops, it stands up straight.
How a bird holds its body can be a good field
mark. For instance, crows and hawks are
about the same size. But most hawks perch
with their bodies straight up and down,
not on a slant, the way crows do.

*American
Robin
page 122*

Bills and beaks

Red Crossbill (female)

Black Skimmer page 77

White Ibis

L ong or short, straight or curved, flattened like a spoon or twisted like a screw, bird bills come in almost every size and shape you can imagine. A bill or beak (you can use either word) is bony inside but is covered with a living, growing layer made up of keratin—the same material as your fingernails.

Being a bill detective

A naturalist can tell a lot about a bird's eating habits just by looking at its bill. If you watch shorebirds along a beach, you'll see how each species uses its beak in a different way. Long-billed Curlews reach deep into the sand for worms, while Semipalmated Sandpipers, with their short bills, probe near the surface. Ruddy Turnstones have stubby beaks with which they flip over rocks to find food. Of course, not all birds have such specialized beaks. Crows, which eat a lot of different foods, have a "generalized" bill shape, suiting many needs.

Roseate Spoonbill page 49

Broad-billed
Hummingbird
(male)

Evening Grosbeak
(male) page 145

American
Crow
page 112

Look—no hands!

Birds have no fingers, so bills are their
tools for finding and eating food. Watch
a cardinal feeding on sunflower seeds;
its heavy beak works like pliers to crack
the tough shells. Chickadees like seeds, too,
but their bills are short and stubby—bad
for crushing seeds. So the chickadee holds
a sunflower seed between its toes and
bangs away until the shell breaks.

Great Blue Heron
page 46

WHAT OTHER BILL-TOOLS DO BIRDS USE?

Woodpeckers have built-in chisels.
The hooked beak of a hawk or owl works
like a knife. Herons and loons have long
spears for grabbing fish, and many small
songbirds have thin bills just right for
reaching into nooks and crannies for
insects. The beak of the crossbill, a large
finch, is just what you'd expect from
its name—its tips overlap at the
end. The crossbill can slip
the tips of its bill inside
a pinecone, pry it
open, and reveal
the seeds.

Long-billed
Curlew

Atlantic Puffin

Yellow-billed
Magpie

Wings and tails

The shape of its wings determines whether a bird flies fast or slow, with lots of flapping or effortless soaring. So when you see a bird in flight, notice the outlines of its wings and how it flies; both are important clues to its identity.

Shape of the wing

Laysan Albatross

Birds such as vultures and hawks, which soar without flapping, have wide wings to catch the lift of rising warm air, and their primaries stick out like fingers on a hand. Very fast fliers, like falcons, swifts, and swallows, have long, pointy wings built for speed. Grouse and pheasants have stubby wings that allow them to take off quickly, dodging trees. But they can't fly for long; because they must flap so hard, they tire quickly. Albatrosses have long, thin wings that let them glide on ocean winds. Most songbirds have short wings, but songbirds that migrate long distances usually have longer primary feathers than those that don't.

TELLING TAILS

Birds steer with their tails and put them to other uses, too. Grouse and Wild Turkeys fan their tails to attract mates. Woodpeckers use them as braces when they lean back on tree trunks. Common Snipe have thin, curved feathers on their tails that make a weird, humming sound in flight to attract females.

Wild Turkey males fanning their tails to display page 89

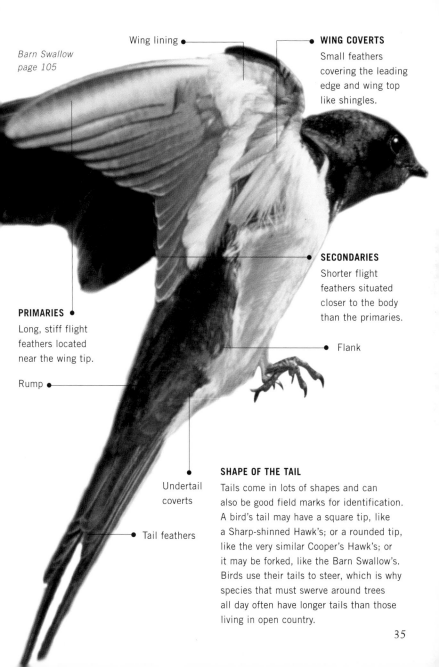

Barn Swallow
page 105

Wing lining

WING COVERTS
Small feathers
covering the leading
edge and wing top
like shingles.

SECONDARIES
Shorter flight
feathers situated
closer to the body
than the primaries.

PRIMARIES
Long, stiff flight
feathers located
near the wing tip.

Flank

Rump

Undertail
coverts

Tail feathers

SHAPE OF THE TAIL

Tails come in lots of shapes and can
also be good field marks for identification.
A bird's tail may have a square tip, like
a Sharp-shinned Hawk's; or a rounded tip,
like the very similar Cooper's Hawk's; or
it may be forked, like the Barn Swallow's.
Birds use their tails to steer, which is why
species that must swerve around trees
all day often have longer tails than those
living in open country.

Why do birds sing?

Birds sing to mark their territory and to attract mates. As though they were posting "No Trespassing" signs around their nests, birds sing songs that others of their species recognize and respect. The singing sounds beautiful and lighthearted but is serious business for the birds.

Yellow-headed Blackbird

Spreading the word

In most bird species, the male does all the singing (one exception is the Northern Cardinal, in which both sexes sing). The time of greatest activity is spring and early summer—the nesting season. Songs not only attract females, they scare away other males. Scientists think birds developed songs to spread their message over a long distance, even in forests where the birds are hidden.

Song and dance routines

Birds of the open country combine songs with courtship flights. If you are in a field where Bobolinks nest, you'll see one male after another bounce into the air, circle on quivering wings, and sing a bubbling version of their name while gliding to earth.

Learning bird songs

Often the only way to tell birds apart is by their songs. To remember the songs, most birders put words to them—for example, the *whichity-whichity-whichity* of a Common Yellowthroat or the American Robin's rolling *cheerily-cheery-me*. But not all birds sing their own songs. Some are mimics, imitating the songs of other species. Northern Mockingbirds, Brown Thrashers, Gray Catbirds, starlings, and Yellow-breasted Chats are all mimics; a single Brown Thrasher may sing 1,000 different songs.

Western Meadowlark

TWO NOTES AT ONCE

Bird song comes from an organ in the throat called the syrinx, which has two sides that vibrate. Some birds, like Wood Thrushes, can sing two different notes at the same time.

HOW DOES A BIRD KNOW WHAT TO SING?

Scientists believe it's partly instinct and partly learned—when a young bird hears an adult singing its species' song, something is triggered in its brain, allowing the youngster to sing the same melody.

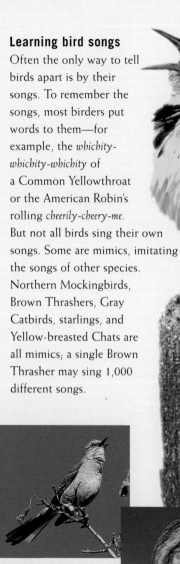

Northern Mockingbird (top) page 124
Song Sparrow (bottom) page 134

37

Bird ranges

An individual bird's home range, or territory, is the patch of land that it uses every day and often defends against intruders of its species. The range of an entire species, on the other hand, is everywhere that sort of bird is found. That's the kind of range you will see indicated on the range maps in the identification section of this book.

House Wren page 116

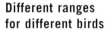

Brown Pelican (page 54) and its range map

HOME SWEET HOME
Migratory birds, such as wrens, have home ranges where they nest and where they spend the winter. Scientists have found that they usually come back to the same ranges year after year.

LARGE OR SMALL, IT'S HOME!
A pair of Golden Eagles will hunt over a range of more than 100 square miles, while a Least Flycatcher's territory may be less than a quarter-acre.

Golden Eagle

Different ranges for different birds

The range map of a Brown Pelican shows that it lives on the coast from New Jersey to Texas and up the California coast. Migratory birds have summer ranges and winter ranges, which may overlap. Song Sparrows are found in summer across Canada, and in winter across much of the South. But elsewhere in the United States, they live year-round.

Where do birds live?

Most birds are not found throughout the ranges shown on their range maps. A particular species usually sticks to certain habitats within its range—places that provide the kinds of food and shelter it needs to survive. For example, the Pileated Woodpecker's range extends throughout the entire eastern United States, central Canada, and the Pacific Northwest, but it is found only in areas where there are mature forests within this range.

WOODLANDS

Forests are good places for birds. Some live only in deciduous forests in which trees lose their leaves in winter, while others prefer conifer forests of pine or spruce. Typical forest birds: Great Horned Owl, Downy Woodpecker, Blue Jay, Hermit Thrush, Red-eyed Vireo, Yellow-rumped Warbler, Red Crossbill.

MOUNTAINS

Life is hard on tall mountains. At high altitudes trees become short and twisted from the wind, and the peaks themselves are covered only with low-growing plants. A few birds live at these heights, although many fly down to the valleys in winter. Typical mountain birds: Golden Eagle, White-tailed Ptarmigan, Clark's Nutcracker, Common Raven, American Pipit, Rosy Finch.

Where do birds live?

DESERTS

Deserts are located where rainfall is very low and doesn't occur often. There are four deserts in the United States, all in the Southwest and West—the Sonoran, Chihuahuan, Mojave, and Great Basin. Typical desert birds: White-winged Dove, Greater Roadrunner, Chihuahuan Raven, Curve-billed Thrasher, Red-tailed Hawk, Gilded Flicker.

CITIES AND SUBURBS

Even large cities have wild birds, such as Peregrine Falcons, which nest on skyscrapers and hunt for pigeons. Nighthawks also nest on rooftops, and Chimney Swifts, in unused chimneys. City parks and suburban yards are good places to look for birds. Typical city birds: Canada Goose, Rock Dove, Chimney Swift, American Robin, European Starling, House Finch, House Sparrow.

Peregrine Falcon page 83

WETLANDS

Among the best habitats for birds are marshes, swamps, and tidal marshes. Birds also gather on ponds, lakes, and rivers during migration. Typical birds: Pied-billed Grebe, Green Heron, Great Blue Heron, Canada Goose, Mallard, Osprey, Clapper Rail, American Coot, Greater Yellowlegs, Black Tern, Tree Swallow, Marsh Wren, Red-winged Blackbird.

Pied-billed Grebe page 52

ODDS, ENDS, AND EDGES

A sharp-eyed naturalist will notice that there are habitats within habitats—like a swampy area in a forest or a small grove of trees by a prairie stream—that often have unusual species of birds. Another good place to look is where habitats, like a field and woodlands or a marsh and drier land, meet. Known as edge habitats, they have birds from each habitat living together.

GRASSLANDS

In the middle of North America are the Great Plains—fertile tallgrass prairie in the Midwest, and low, dry shortgrass prairie closer to the Rocky Mountains. Much of the

prairie has been replaced by farm fields, but many of the birds remain. Typical birds: Killdeer, Greater Prairie-chicken, Mourning Dove, Burrowing Owl, Scissor-tailed Flycatcher, Dickcissel, Eastern Meadowlark, American Goldfinch.

Burrowing Owl
page 95

SEASHORES

Seashores can be gentle sand beaches, rocky cliffs, or tidal marshes. Cliffs make ideal nesting sites for many seabirds, including puffins, gannets, and gulls. Typical birds: Common Loon (winter), Brown Pelican, Common Eider (rocky coasts), Black-bellied Plover, Sanderling, Herring Gull, Least Tern, Tufted Puffin (cliffs).

Tufted Puffins
page 78

41

Endangered birds

Snail Kite

Birds play a vital role in the web of life. They eat countless insects and rodents, helping to keep the numbers of these creatures under control. They serve as food for many animals. They pollinate plants and spread seeds. They inspire us with their beauty and fascinating behavior. You can join people who are working to save our endangered birds and help make a difference. See the list of organizations on page 153.

PROTECTING HABITATS is the most important thing humans can do for birds. The Snail Kite of the Florida Everglades and the Kirtland's Warbler, which lives in a small part of Michigan, have very little habitat left for them.

Osprey
page 81

Birds and DDT

In the 1960s, the numbers of Brown Pelicans, Bald Eagles, Ospreys, and Peregrine Falcons in North America were declining. Scientists found that DDT, a pesticide, was getting into the birds' bodies through their food. The DDT made the birds' eggshells too thin. Since 1972, when DDT was banned, the populations of these birds have increased.

PITY THE CALIFORNIA CONDOR

The California Condor used to live along the Pacific coast as well as in the mountains of Southern California, but by the 1940s it survived only in the mountains. Once egg-collecting and illegal shooting were the worst dangers, but today pesticides and too little habitat are the biggest problems. Most California Condors now live in cages, although scientists have returned some to the wild in California and the Grand Canyon.

California Condor

Barely hanging on

Red-cockaded Woodpeckers live only in old pine forests in the Southeast. Whooping Cranes nest only in a single park in Canada and winter in a small part of the Texas coast. Least Terns and Piping Plovers nest on beaches, where dune buggies crush their nests.

Kirtland's Warbler

DISAPPEARING SONGBIRDS

Many naturalists worry that songbirds, such as orioles, warblers, and vireos, aren't as common as they used to be. Scientists blame destruction of the tropical forests, where these birds spend the winter, and of the northern forests, where they nest.

Whooping Crane

Black-crowned Night Heron

Using the field guide

This section features 50 common North American birds and includes brief descriptions of 125 more. Color photographs and details about each bird are included to help you identify it. Birds appearing on a spread together are either related or share some traits or characteristics. Birds pictured are usually males. Males are often more colorful and easier to identify than females. In a few cases females differing from males of a species are also shown.

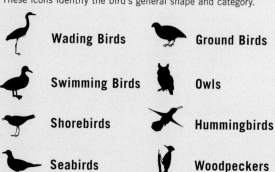

Mountain Bluebird page 121

ICONS

These icons identify the bird's general shape and category.

Wading Birds

Ground Birds

Swimming Birds

Owls

Shorebirds

Hummingbirds

Seabirds

Woodpeckers

Hawks & Eagles

Backyard Birds

When you go out to observe birds, take your binoculars, a notebook and a pencil, and this field guide or the spotter's guide. Also take a buddy with you. Always tell your parents or a grown-up when you are going out. Respect other people's property, and observe the Naturalist's Code of Ethics on page 9.

SHAPE ICON
This icon identifies the featured bird's general shape and category.

NAME
Each bird's common and scientific names appear here.

BOX HEADING
The box heading alerts you to other birds covered in the box that are similar in some way to the main bird on the page. These box headings include: Long-legged Waders, Water Birds, In the Same Family, Look-alikes, Shorebirds, Birds of Prey, Owls, Similar Species, Similar Silhouettes, Songbirds, and Prairie Songbirds.

GREAT BLUE HERON
Ardea herodias

LOOK FOR: A tall, grayish bird with white face, yellow bill, and black on its shoulders, crown, and belly. It has broad wings, a slow wingbeat, and folded neck in flight. A white form lives in Florida but unlike the Great Egret has greenish-yellow legs.
LENGTH: 39–52".

VOICE: A hoarse squawk.

RANGE: **HABITAT:**
• marshes
• swamps
• rivers
• lakes

The Great Blue Heron can stand as still as a statue at the water's edge, waiting and watching for a fish or frog to happen by. The instant one appears, the bird makes a lightning-fast strike with its spear-like bill.

LONG-LEGGED WADERS

GREEN HERON
Butorides virescens
LOOK FOR: A small, dark heron with yellow legs. **LENGTH:** 16–22". **VOICE:** Usually silent. **HABITAT:** Marshes, swamps, streamsides. **RANGE:** Widespread except the Great Plains.

GREAT EGRET
Ardea alba
LOOK FOR: A large, white heron with yellow bill and dark legs. **LENGTH:** 35–41". **VOICE:** Usually silent. **HABITAT:** Marshes, ponds. **RANGE:** Coasts, central United States.

SANDHILL CRANE
Grus canadensis
LOOK FOR: A tall, gray bird with long neck and red cap. **LENGTH:** 34–48". **VOICE:** Loud, low *garooo*. **HABITAT:** Marshes, fields. **RANGE:** Canada, northern prairies, Great Lakes area. Gulf Coast, winter: Gulf to California.

47

IDENTIFICATION CAPSULE
The identification capsule covers all the details you need to identify a bird: color, size, shape, voice, and other field marks discussed in this book.

RANGE AND HABITAT
The range map and habitat listings tell you at a glance whether or not a bird is likely to be in your area. Color coding indicates where a bird can be found at different times of year.

 SUMMER

 WINTER

ALL SEASONS

45

GREAT BLUE HERON
Ardea herodias

The Great Blue Heron can stand as still as a statue at the water's edge, waiting and watching for a fish or frog to happen by. The instant one appears, the bird makes a lightning-fast strike with its spear-like bill.

LOOK FOR: A tall, grayish bird with white face, yellow bill, and black on its shoulders, crown, and belly. It has broad wings, a slow wingbeat, and folded neck in flight. A white form lives in Florida but unlike the Great Egret has greenish-yellow legs.

LENGTH: 39–52".

VOICE: A hoarse squawk.

RANGE:

HABITAT:

- marshes
- swamps
- rivers
- lakes

GREEN HERON
Butorides virescens

LOOK FOR: A small, dark heron with yellow legs. **LENGTH:** 16–22". **VOICE:** Usually silent. **HABITAT:** Marshes, swamps, stream-sides. **RANGE:** Widespread except the Great Plains.

GREAT EGRET
Ardea alba

LOOK FOR: A large, white heron with yellow bill and dark legs. **LENGTH:** 35–41". **VOICE:** Usually silent. **HABITAT:** Marshes, ponds. **RANGE:** Coasts, central United States.

SANDHILL CRANE
Grus canadensis

LOOK FOR: A tall, gray bird with long neck and red cap. **LENGTH:** 34–48". **VOICE:** Loud, low *garooo*. **HABITAT:** Marshes, fields. **RANGE:** Canada, northern prairies, Great Lakes area; Gulf Coast; winter: Gulf to California.

47

The long, down-curved bill of the Glossy Ibis is a handy tool, used to probe shallow waters for crayfish, crabs, insects, and snakes. This ibis almost always nests in colonies with herons and other large wading birds.

LOOK FOR: A large, reddish-bronze bird with glossy green wings and long bill. Juvenile is dull brown.

LENGTH: 22–25".

VOICE: Usually silent; sometimes bleats like sheep.

RANGE:

HABITAT:

- coastal marshes

AMERICAN BITTERN
Botaurus lentiginosus

LOOK FOR: A brown-and-white streaked bird with white throat and yellowish bill. Well camouflaged, hard to see. **LENGTH:** 23–34". **VOICE:** *Pump-a-lunk.* **HABITAT:** Marshes. **RANGE:** Widespread.

ROSEATE SPOONBILL
Ajaia ajaja

LOOK FOR: A bright, pink-and-white bird with a spoon-shaped bill. **LENGTH:** 30–32". **VOICE:** Usually silent. **HABITAT:** Mangroves. **RANGE:** Coasts of Florida, Texas, and Louisiana.

WOOD STORK
Mycteria americana

LOOK FOR: A large, white bird with a long bill and featherless head and neck. Endangered. **LENGTH:** 40–44". **VOICE:** Usually silent. **HABITAT:** Swamps; mangroves. **RANGE:** Florida and Georgia.

49

COMMON LOON
Gavia immer

The call of the Common Loon sounds like wild laughter, giving rise to the expression "crazy as a loon." A superb swimmer and diver, the loon shuffles clumsily on land because its legs are set far back on its body. It can take flight only from water. There are fewer and fewer loons as a result of water pollution, noisy boats, and lakeshore development.

Look for: In summer, black head and neck with white bands on neck; black back with white spots. In winter, dark gray with white throat and breast.

Length: 28–36".

Voice: A quavering, laugh-like wail; also a sad yodel. Heard mostly on summer nights.

Range: **Habitat:**

- forests
- lakes
- rivers
- oceans in winter

RED-THROATED LOON
Gavia stellata

Look for: In summer, gray head and neck, red throat, black back dotted with white. In winter, similar to Common Loon, but smaller and paler. **Length:** 24–27". **Voice:** A variety of calls, often *ga-ga-ga* in flight. **Habitat:** Summer: Arctic tundra and coasts; winter: ocean. **Range:** Pacific, Florida, and Atlantic coasts.

NORTHERN GANNET
Morus bassanus

Look for: Adult: white with black wing tips and orange-tinted head. Juveniles: gray speckled with white; similar to loon. **Length:** 35–40". **Voice:** Usually silent. **Habitat:** Open sea, rocky islands. **Range:** Atlantic Coast.

PIED-BILLED GREBE
Podilymbus podiceps

This grebe can dive so fast that it was nicknamed "Hell-diver" and "Water-witch." It can escape enemies by gradually sinking, until only its bill and nostrils are above the surface—like a submarine with its periscope up.

LOOK FOR: A brown, duck-like water bird with short, cone-shaped bill ringed in black during summer. In winter, the bill is yellow or gray without a ring.

LENGTH: 12–15".

VOICE: *Cow-cow-cow-cow-cow* and *coup, coup, coup* notes.

RANGE: **HABITAT:**

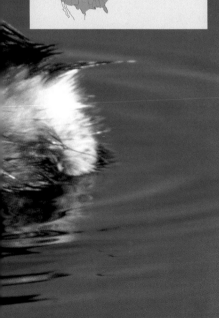

- marshes
- ponds
- bays

HORNED GREBE
Podiceps auritus

LOOK FOR: In summer, very obvious brownish-yellow ear tufts. **LENGTH:** 12–15". **VOICE:** Usually silent. **HABITAT:** Marshes, lakes; winter: coasts. **RANGE:** Northern lakes; all coasts.

WESTERN GREBE
Aechmophorus occidentalis

LOOK FOR: Swan-like neck with white on front. **LENGTH:** 22–29". **VOICE:** Usually silent. **HABITAT:** Marshy lakes, coastal bays. **RANGE:** Western lakes; winter: Pacific and Gulf coasts.

EARED GREBE
Podiceps nigricollis

LOOK FOR: In summer, black-crested head with golden ear tufts. **LENGTH:** 12–14". **VOICE:** Usually silent. **HABITAT:** Marshes, lakes, ocean, bays. **RANGE:** Western lakes; winter: Pacific and Gulf coasts.

53

BROWN PELICAN
Pelecanus occidentalis

Diving from great heights, the pelican plunges headfirst into the water and scoops up fish into the expandable pouch beneath its bill. When the water drains out, the pelican throws its head back and swallows. Brown Pelicans were once in grave danger due to the effects of pesticides. Thanks to conservation efforts, these amazing birds are now often seen along our shores.

DOUBLE-CRESTED CORMORANT
Phalacrocorax auritus

LOOK FOR: A large black bird with crooked neck and orange throat patch. **LENGTH:** 30–35". **HABITAT:** Coasts, rivers, lakes. **RANGE:** East and West coasts, inland waters.

ANHINGA
Anhinga anhinga

LOOK FOR: A large black bird with a long, thin, S-shaped neck and pointed bill. **LENGTH:** 34–36". **VOICE:** Usually silent. **HABITAT:** Ponds, lakes, rivers, and swamps. **RANGE:** Southeast and Gulf states.

MAGNIFICENT FRIGATEBIRD
Fregata magnificens

LOOK FOR: A large black, soaring seabird with pointed wings and forked tail. Males have red throat pouch. **LENGTH:** 38–40". **VOICE:** Usually silent. **HABITAT:** Ocean. **RANGE:** Southeast and Gulf coasts.

LOOK FOR: A very large, stocky bird with gray-brown body, long bill, and pouch under bill. Adults have light yellow crown. In summer, back of neck is chestnut brown; in winter, changes to white. Flocks fly in straight lines, often gliding just above the water.

LENGTH: 45–54".

VOICE: Usually quiet; low croaks at nest.

RANGE:

HABITAT:

- coasts
- beaches
- bays

55

CANADA GOOSE
Branta canadensis

Canada Geese vary greatly in size. Some are a bit larger than an average duck; others are twice that size. They can be seen flying in a V-shaped formation when they migrate in the spring and fall. Today, however, there is a growing population of year-round residents in suburban areas.

SNOW GOOSE
Chen caerulescens

LOOK FOR: A pure white goose with black wing tips; pink bill has black "lip." (Can also be dark gray.) **LENGTH:** 25–31". **VOICE:** *Honk-honk!* **HABITAT:** Saltwater marshes, bays. **RANGE:** Summer: Arctic; winter: California, Gulf, and Mid-Atlantic coasts.

TUNDRA SWAN
Cygnus columbianus

LOOK FOR: A large, white bird with black bill. **LENGTH:** 48–55". **VOICE:** *Hoo-ho-hoo.* **HABITAT:** Tundra, lakes, bays. **RANGE:** Summer: Arctic; winter: Pacific and Mid-Atlantic coasts, Great Lakes area.

LOOK FOR: A brownish body with black head, long black neck, and broad white chinstrap extending onto cheeks. Pale brown breast; short black tail.

LENGTH: 22–45".

VOICE: Large geese honk, small geese cackle.

RANGE:

HABITAT:

- marshes
- lakes
- ponds
- fields
- lawns

MALLARD
Anas platyrhynchos

LOOK FOR: Male has a green head and neck, white neck ring and purple breast, and gray wings and body. Orange legs and yellow bill are very noticeable. The female is speckled brown with an orange-and-black speckled bill.

LENGTH: 18–24".

VOICE: Female: loud *quack*.
Male: quiet.

RANGE:

HABITAT:

- rivers
- lakes
- marshes

The most commonly found duck in the world, the Mallard numbers nearly 10 million in North America alone. The strong and fast-flying Mallard is the forefather of the domestic white duck and frequently breeds with it.

FEMALE

WOOD DUCK
Aix sponsa

LOOK FOR: Male: green, purple, blue, with white on face and chin. **LENGTH:** 17–20". **VOICE:** Female: *weeeek* or *oooeek;* Male: high whistle. **HABITAT:** Swamps, marshes, streams, and ponds. **RANGE:** Pacific Coast and eastern half of United States.

NORTHERN SHOVELER
Anas clypeata

LOOK FOR: Large, shovel-shaped bill. Male: green head that is flattish in shape and white body with reddish flanks. Female: patchy brown with blue-gray shoulders. **LENGTH:** 17–20". **VOICE:** Low chuckle or quack. **HABITAT:** Marshes, prairie potholes. **RANGE:** Widespread.

AMERICAN WIGEON
Anas americana

Nicknamed "baldpate" for the male's whitish crown and forehead, this duck is often seen in the company of other diving birds, whose food it snatches. When alarmed, the wigeon rises straight up out of the water with a rattling of wings.

LOOK FOR: The male has a white forehead and a green patch behind the eyes, brownish body with bronze sides, and speckled head.

LENGTH: 18–23".

VOICE: Male: soft whistle. Female: *quack*.

RANGE:

HABITAT:

- lakes
- marshes
- protected coasts

NORTHERN PINTAIL
Anas acuta

LOOK FOR: Male: brown head with a white stripe; white neck; pointed tail. **LENGTH:** 25–30". **VOICE:** Male: piping whistle. Female: *quack.* **HABITAT:** Marshes, ponds. **RANGE:** Widespread.

BLUE-WINGED TEAL
Anas discors

LOOK FOR: Blue wing patches. Male: small white patch on face. **LENGTH:** 14–16". **VOICE:** Male: squeaky *peeps.* Female: *quack.* **HABITAT:** Ponds, marshes, lakes. **RANGE:** Widespread.

BUFFLEHEAD
Bucephala albeola

LOOK FOR: White body, triangular white patch on back of male's head. **LENGTH:** 13–15". **VOICE:** Male: squeaky whistle. Female: hoarse *quack.* **HABITAT:** Bays, large lakes. **RANGE:** Widespread.

61

COMMON GOLDENEYE
Bucephala clangula

LOOK FOR: The male is a black-and-white duck with a dark green head, and a round, white spot near the bill. The eyes are bright yellow. Female is gray, with a dark brown head. Both the male and female have large heads.

LENGTH: 16–20".

VOICE: Male: quiet, except whistles during courtship. Female: *quack*.

RANGE:

HABITAT:

- lakes in summer
- coastal bays in winter

When the Common Golden-eye flies, its wings make a whistling sound, giving this duck the nickname "Whistler." Bird-watchers, listening for this sound, can identify the Common Golden-eye even when they cannot see it.

GREATER SCAUP
Aythya marila

LOOK FOR: Male: gray body, white sides, glossy greenish-black head, and pale blue bill. Female: brown with white patch on face. **LENGTH:** 15–20". **VOICE:** Usually silent. **HABITAT:** Lakes, bays, and open ocean; winter: saltwater bays. **RANGE:** Pacific and Atlantic coasts in winter.

RING-NECKED DUCK
Aythya collaris

LOOK FOR: White ring on bill. Male: glossy purple head, white patch between breast and sides. **LENGTH:** 14–18". **VOICE:** Usually silent. **HABITAT:** Wooded lakes, rivers, ponds. **RANGE:** Widespread.

63

AMERICAN COOT
Fulica americana

Although the American Coot is a superb swimmer, it is plump and has difficulty taking flight, pattering across the water to gain speed. It feeds on aquatic animals and plants, often snatching uprooted plants brought up by Canvasbacks and other ducks. Coots swim in open water, often in large groups.

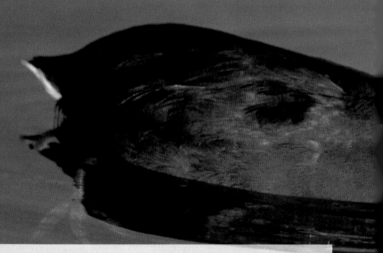

LOOK FOR: A slate-gray, black-headed bird with a white bill. Head and neck are black. Toes are lobed (separate) rather than webbed. Juveniles are paler gray below; bill silvery.

LENGTH: 15".

VOICE: Grating *kuk* notes.

RANGE:

HABITAT:
- marshes
- ponds

COMMON MOORHEN
Gallinula chloropus

LOOK FOR: A gray bird with a bright red shield on its forehead and a yellow-tipped red bill. The feet are yellow-green. Like coots, moorhens bob their heads up and down while swimming. Previously called "Common Gallinule." **LENGTH:** 14". **VOICE:** Squawks and croaks. **HABITAT:** Freshwater marshes, cattail-edged ponds. **RANGE:** Widespread in the East, South, and Southwest.

SORA
Porzana carolina

LOOK FOR: A chicken-shaped bird with a brownish back and gray breast with black-and-white bands underneath. Face is black with a yellow bill. Large feet with long toes. **LENGTH:** 8–10". **VOICE:** Musical whinny; also whistled *ker-wee, ker-wee.* **HABITAT:** Freshwater marshes; winter: saltwater marshes. **RANGE:** Widespread.

65

KILLDEER
Charadrius vociferus

The Killdeer has a unique way of distracting predators. When it feels that its nest is threatened, the adult will pretend to be injured, stumbling along the ground while dragging one of its wings. When the potential attacker is lured away from the nest, the Killdeer suddenly flies off.

LOOK FOR: Adult is dark brown above, white below, with two black chest bands. The legs are pinkish gray. Killdeer have red eye rings. The chicks have one black chest band.

LENGTH: 9–11".

VOICE: High-pitched *kill-dee*.

RANGE:

HABITAT:
- farms
- fields
- golf courses

SEMIPALMATED PLOVER
Charadrius semipalmatus

LOOK FOR: A small bird, brown above, white below, with one black band on chest. The orange bill has a dark tip. This plover is partially web-footed (*palmate* means "webbed"). **LENGTH:** 6–8".
VOICE: A rising whistle, *chu-wee*. **HABITAT:** Beaches, lakeshores, marshes. **RANGE:** Winter: Gulf Coast, coasts of California and southeastern states; breeds in the Arctic.

BLACK-BELLIED PLOVER
Pluvialis squatarola

LOOK FOR: In summer: speckled black and white above, black below. In winter: gray with white below and on face. **LENGTH:** 10–13". **VOICE:** Whistling *queeooooee*. **HABITAT:** Beaches, mudflats, coastal marshes. **RANGE:** Coastlines; breeds in the Arctic.

67

GREATER YELLOWLEGS
Tringa melanoleuca

This species of shorebird is found in small flocks feeding in shallow water on fish, worms, and insects. It moves about quickly, bobbing its head and tail. Like a good watchdog, the Greater Yellowlegs sounds a loud alarm when danger approaches, alerting birds in the area. Then the whole flock may take flight.

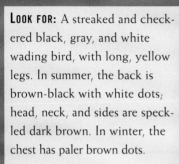

LOOK FOR: A streaked and checkered black, gray, and white wading bird, with long, yellow legs. In summer, the back is brown-black with white dots; head, neck, and sides are speckled dark brown. In winter, the chest has paler brown dots.

LENGTH: 12–15".

VOICE: Three or more whistles, *whew-whew-whew*.

RANGE:

HABITAT:
- marshes
- mudflats
- flooded fields

BLACK-NECKED STILT
Himantopus mexicanus

LOOK FOR: A slender black-and-white bird with long, red legs. Bill is straight, unlike avocet's. **LENGTH:** 13–16". **VOICE:** Loud *kep-kep-kep*. **HABITAT:** Marshes, bays. **RANGE:** Coastlines and some western states.

AMERICAN OYSTERCATCHER
Haematopus palliatus

LOOK FOR: A black-and-white shorebird with long, red bill and pink legs. **LENGTH:** 17–21". **VOICE:** Sharp, repeated *cleep!* **HABITAT:** Beaches, salt marshes. **RANGE:** Atlantic and Gulf coasts.

AMERICAN AVOCET
Recurvirostra americana

LOOK FOR: Long legs. Head and neck cinnamon colored; whitish in winter. Bill curves up. **LENGTH:** 16–20". **VOICE:** Loud *pleek*. **HABITAT:** Coasts, marshes. **RANGE:** West, Atlantic and Gulf coasts.

69

COMMON SNIPE
Gallinago gallinago

The Common Snipe performs a remarkable aerial courtship display over its nesting area, climbing high into the air and then power-diving, making a strange winnowing sound as its outer tail feathers vibrate in the air. The snipe flies in a zigzag pattern.

LOOK FOR: A long-billed, short-legged brown bird with stripes on back and head. The tail is reddish.

LENGTH: 10½–11½".

VOICE: Rasping *scaip* when alarmed; whistles *wheet, wheet* at the nest.

RANGE:

HABITAT:
- wet meadows
- marshes

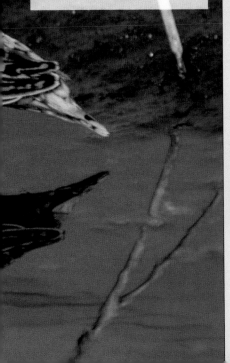

WILLET
Catoptrophorus semipalmatus

LOOK FOR: A large, gray or brownish-gray bird, with a bold white stripe on black wings in flight. **LENGTH:** 15". **VOICE:** *Pill-will-willet.* **HABITAT:** Marshes, beaches, wet prairies. **RANGE:** Coasts, prairie states.

SHORT-BILLED DOWITCHER
Limnodromus griseus

LOOK FOR: Reddish in summer, gray in winter. White rump seen during flight. Long bill. **LENGTH:** 12". **VOICE:** *Tu-tu-tu.* **HABITAT:** Marshes, tidal flats. **RANGE:** Winter: Southwest and Southeast coasts.

AMERICAN WOODCOCK
Scolopax minor

LOOK FOR: Long bill and large, bulging eyes. **LENGTH:** 11". **VOICE:** A buzzy *peent.* **HABITAT:** Wetlands, woods, and thickets. **RANGE:** Eastern half of United States.

Sanderlings look like wind-up toys as they scurry after retreating waves. They rapidly and repeatedly stab the beach with their bills, searching for their favorite foods—crustaceans, worms, and mollusks—that have been uncovered by the surf.

LOOK FOR: A small shorebird with black bill and legs, and a bold white wing stripe. In summer, it is reddish above and white below, with a reddish head. In winter, the red is replaced by a speckled gray.

LENGTH: 7–8".

VOICE: *Kip* sound in flight.

RANGE:

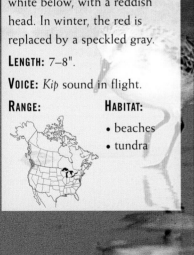

HABITAT:
- beaches
- tundra

LEAST SANDPIPER
Calidris minutilla

LOOK FOR: A very small bird that is brown above, with a streaked breast and yellow or greenish legs. Short, thin beak. It is the smallest American shorebird. **LENGTH:** 6". **VOICE:** High *kreep*. **HABITAT:** Marshes, bogs, grassy pools, flooded fields. **RANGE:** Breeds in the Arctic; winter: Southeast, Southwest, and coasts.

SPOTTED SANDPIPER
Actitis macularia

LOOK FOR: A slim, brown shorebird with white, spotted breast and underparts. Tail tips as it walks. **LENGTH:** 7½". **VOICE:** Loud *peet-weet*. **HABITAT:** Coastal and inland waters. **RANGE:** Widespread.

HERRING GULL
Larus argentatus

A scavenger that eats almost anything it finds, this widespread gull even likes to feast at garbage dumps far inland. The Herring Gull deliberately drops clams on rocks or pavement in order to open them. It also eats fish, garbage, insects, and the eggs and young of other birds.

LOOK FOR: A mostly white bird with pale gray back and wings. Legs and feet are pink or flesh-colored, and the bill is yellow with a red dot. In flight, wing tips show small white spots. Like most gulls, juveniles are brownish.

JUVENILE

LENGTH: 23–26".

VOICE: Squealing *ke-yah;* also *ee-you.*

RANGE:

HABITAT:
- seacoasts
- oceans
- lakes
- rivers

LAUGHING GULL
Larus atricilla

LOOK FOR: Dark-gray back, white underparts. In summer, it has a black head. **LENGTH:** 15–17". **VOICE:** Loud, high-pitched *ha-ha-ha-ha.* **HABITAT:** Seacoasts, saltwater marshes. **RANGE:** Atlantic and Gulf coasts.

RING-BILLED GULL
Larus delawarensis

LOOK FOR: Similar to Herring Gull but smaller. White head, breast, and underparts, with light gray back and wings. Has dark ring near tip of yellow bill. Yellow legs. **LENGTH:** 18–20". **VOICE:** Loud *kree, kree, kree.* **HABITAT:** Lakes, rivers, bays, coasts. **RANGE:** Widespread.

75

The Common Tern (a member of the gull family) dives headfirst into the water, then flies away with a fish in its bill. Common Terns vigorously defend their colonies and will dive at—and sometimes strike—humans who disturb their nest areas.

LOOK FOR: A white-bodied, gull-like bird with light gray back and wings and a black cap. Red bill is straight with a black tip. The tail is deeply forked. Smaller than most gulls.

LENGTH: 13–16".

VOICE: Short *kip;* drawn-out *tee-arrr.*

RANGE:

HABITAT:
- lakes
- ponds
- beaches
- coastal waters

BLACK SKIMMER
Rynchops niger

LOOK FOR: Bill is red with black tip. Flies over the water, skimming the surface for fish with its large lower bill. Body is black on top, white below; red legs. **LENGTH:** 18". **VOICE:** Short barks. **HABITAT:** Sandy beaches, shallow bays. **RANGE:** Eastern and southern coasts.

ROYAL TERN
Sterna maxima

LOOK FOR: A black-capped tern with gray wings and back; larger than the Common Tern and doesn't have black tip on orange-red bill. **LENGTH:** 18–21". **VOICE:** *Keeer.* **HABITAT:** Sandy beaches by salt water. **RANGE:** Eastern and southern coasts.

77

TUFTED PUFFIN
Fratercula cirrhata

A strange-looking seabird, this puffin is instantly recognizable in summer by the parrotlike, orange-red bill and the long, curved, yellow plumes that extend from behind each eye. In winter no plumes adorn it, and its beak molts, becoming smaller and duller.

LOOK FOR: In summer, mostly black with a white face. Big red bill has a yellow base. Wings are short and the large webbed feet are set far back on the body. Eyes are yellow with a red ring. In winter, the puffin is all gray with a dull reddish bill.

LENGTH: 14½–15½".

VOICE: Growl-like *errr*.

RANGE:

HABITAT:
- ocean
- sea cliffs

MARBLED MURRELET
Brachyramphus marmoratus

LOOK FOR: In late winter and early spring (before the breeding season), this black-and-white seabird molts its feathers and becomes grayish brown with bars.
LENGTH: 9–10½". **VOICE:** Shrill *meer-meer-meer*. **HABITAT:** Rocky coasts; nests in mountains. **RANGE:** Pacific Northwest Coast to central California.

COMMON MURRE
Uria aalge

LOOK FOR: A black-and-white penguin-like bird. In summer has blackish-brown head and face; in winter (above) lower part of face becomes white.
LENGTH: 17". **VOICE:** Low *murrrr*. **HABITAT:** Rocky cliffs and ledges. **RANGE:** Arctic, Pacific, and North Atlantic coasts.

BALD EAGLE
Haliaeetus leucocephalus

I n mid-November 3,000 to 4,000 Bald Eagles gather along a 10-mile stretch of Alaska's Chilkat River to feed on spawning salmon. Once threatened with extinction in the lower 48 states, our national bird has been making a slow comeback, thanks to conservation efforts.

LOOK FOR: A large, dark brown eagle with a snow-white head and a hooked, yellow bill. Juveniles are all brown.

IN FLIGHT

LENGTH: 30–40".

VOICE: Harsh cackle.

RANGE:

HABITAT:
- wetlands
- lakes
- rivers
- coastlines

OSPREY
Pandion haliaetus

LOOK FOR: Hunts fish by hovering over the water. Brown above and white below, with a dark line on the side of its head. **LENGTH:** 21–24". **VOICE:** Loud whistle. **HABITAT:** Wetlands and seacoasts, especially coastal marshes. **RANGE:** Northern half of continent, and southern coasts.

TURKEY VULTURE
Cathartes aura

LOOK FOR: A large black bird with small, reddish head. Holds long wings in V while in flight. **LENGTH:** 25–32". **VOICE:** Silent, except grunts and hisses when threatened. **HABITAT:** Open country, forests. **RANGE:** Widespread.

81

RED-TAILED HAWK
Buteo jamaicensis

The Red-tail divides its time between perching in trees and soaring, always looking for prey, such as small rodents or reptiles. Like other buteos (soaring hawks), it drifts in wide circles in the sky.

LOOK FOR: Brown above, white below, often with dark streaks on belly. May be all brown in West.

The tail is brown in juveniles, orangish in adults.

LENGTH: 18–25".

VOICE: *Keeear* scream descending from high to low.

RANGE: **HABITAT:**

- open country
- forests

RED-SHOULDERED HAWK
Buteo lineatus

LOOK FOR: A large hawk with white bars on long wings, reddish shoulders, and banded tail.
LENGTH: 16–24".
VOICE: Loud, descending scream. **HABITAT:** Swampy woods, bogs. **RANGE:** Eastern United States, California.

NORTHERN HARRIER
Circus cyaneus

LOOK FOR: Male: pale gray with long tail and white patch on rump. Female: brown, streaked below. **LENGTH:** 16–24". **VOICE:** Usually quiet. **HABITAT:** Marshes, open fields. **RANGE:** Widespread.

PEREGRINE FALCON
Falco peregrinus

LOOK FOR: Pointed wings and black head and cheeks. Saved from extinction by a ban on particular pesticides.
LENGTH: 15–21".
VOICE: *Kak kak* at nest. **HABITAT:** Open country, cities. **RANGE:** Coastlines and mountains.

83

The smallest falcon, the kestrel often hovers in midair, looking for mice, sparrows, or large insects. It nests in holes in trees, on cliffs, or on buildings. Families stay together for months after babies learn to fly.

LOOK FOR: Two thin, black sideburns on white face.

The male has reddish back, blue-gray wings and a black band at end of tail. The female has reddish wings and back.

LENGTH: 9–12".

VOICE: High *klee klee klee.*

RANGE:

HABITAT:
- fields
- forest clearings
- farms
- deserts
- towns

SHARP-SHINNED HAWK
Accipiter striatus

LOOK FOR: A fast, small hawk with a slender body, rounded wings, and a long, squared-off tail. Hunts small birds. Often seen soaring at migration lookout sites.
LENGTH: 10–14". **VOICE:** High *kek kek kek kek.*
HABITAT: Woods. **RANGE:** Widespread.

COOPER'S HAWK
Accipiter cooperii

LOOK FOR: Crow-sized. Grayish above, lighter with reddish bars below. **LENGTH:** 14–20". **VOICE:** Loud *kak kak kak kak.*
HABITAT: Forests. **RANGE:** Widespread.

NORTHERN BOBWHITE
Colinus virginianus

The Northern Bobwhite is named for its well-known *bob-white* call given by males in mating season. Spends most of its time on the ground gathered in family groups or "coveys" of one to two dozen birds. Runs for cover and then freezes and "flushes" when frightened.

LOOK FOR: A small, brown-and-white speckled bird. The male's face is black-and-white, female's white with yellow-brown.

LENGTH: 8–11".

VOICE: Clear whistled *bob-white*.

RANGE:

HABITAT:
- brushy fields
- farmlands
- open woods

RUFFED GROUSE
Bonasa umbellus

LOOK FOR: A reddish- or grayish-brown bird, with dark neck ruff and a tail that fans out during male mating display. **LENGTH:** 16–19". **VOICE:** Female: *coos* and *clucks*. Male: sound of drumming with wings. **HABITAT:** Broadleaf and mixed forests. **RANGE:** Mostly northern regions and mountains.

CALIFORNIA QUAIL
Callipepla californica

LOOK FOR: A stocky, brownish bird; belly has scale-like markings. Curved plume on head. **LENGTH:** 9–11". **VOICE:** *Ca-caa-co*, also clucking. **HABITAT:** Brushy areas, deserts, suburbs. **RANGE:** Pacific Northwest, California.

87

RING-NECKED PHEASANT
Phasianus colchicus

FEMALE

Originally a native of China, this bird has thrived in the farmlands of North America. The pheasant takes off with rapid and noisy wingbeats, and then glides to cover.

WILD TURKEY
Meleagris gallopavo

LOOK FOR: Male: naked red, white, and blue head, with black beard on breast.
LENGTH: 36–48". **VOICE:** *Gobble, gobble, gobble.*
HABITAT: Forests. **RANGE:** Widespread; increasing in the East.

GREATER PRAIRIE-CHICKEN
Tympanuchus cupido

LOOK FOR: Grayish-brown-and-white bars on body. Male: black neck feathers; orange air sacs inflated in courtship. **LENGTH:** 16–18".
VOICE: Booming calls in courtship. **HABITAT:** Native grasslands. **RANGE:** Great Plains.

GREATER ROADRUNNER
Geococcyx californianus

LOOK FOR: Long tail and crested head, rapid runner with sturdy legs. Runs with neck and tail outstretched. Short stops.
LENGTH: 24". **VOICE:** *Coos, oohs,* and *clucks.*
HABITAT: Desert. **RANGE:** Southwest.

LOOK FOR: A chickenlike, reddish-bronze bird with very long and pointed tail feathers. The male has bright red skin around its eyes, an iridescent green head, and a white ring around its neck. Females and juveniles are a speckled buff brown.

LENGTH: Male: 30–36". Female: 21–24".

VOICE: Loud *kaw kawk.*

RANGE:

HABITAT:
- farmlands
- meadows
- grasslands

89

MOURNING DOVE
Zenaida macroura

This common dove is found in many habitats. It has a well-known, mournful call, and its wings make a distinctive whistling sound when it takes flight. Adults nourish their young by coughing up a partially digested food mixture (called pigeon milk) and feeding it to their chicks until they are ready to eat insects and seeds on their own.

LOOK FOR: A gray-brown bird with a small head, a short black bill, a long, tapered tail, and short red legs. The male has blue-gray on his cap and the back of his neck.

LENGTH: 11–13".

VOICE: Mournful *coo, who-o coo.*

RANGE:

HABITAT:
- fields
- gardens
- parks

ROCK DOVE
Columba livia

LOOK FOR: Our most common pigeon.
Color varies: white to rusty to blue-gray
to black; rounded tail and white rump.
LENGTH: 13½". **VOICE:** Deep cooing. **HABITAT:**
Cities, suburbs, farms. **RANGE:** Widespread.

BAND-TAILED PIGEON
Columba fasciata

LOOK FOR: Dark gray with white band on
neck; yellow bill with black tip. **LENGTH:**
14–15½". **VOICE:** Low-pitched *whoohoo*.
HABITAT: Mountain forests. **RANGE:** Pacific
and Southwest states.

COMMON GROUND-DOVE
Columbina passerina

LOOK FOR: A small, brown dove with red on
its wings. **LENGTH:** 6½". **VOICE:** Soft rising
coos. **HABITAT:** Fields, gardens, roadsides.
RANGE: Southernmost United States.

91

A large, powerful, and aggressive bird, the Great Horned Owl's menu extends from insects, frogs, and mice to rabbits and skunks, as well as other birds. This "tiger of the woods" even eats porcupines and house cats.

LOOK FOR: Has fluffy ear tufts spaced wide apart and yellow eyes. Body varies in color from pale gray in the Arctic to dark brown. Underparts are speckled and streaked. Throat is white. The facial mask, a rusty brown, is ringed in black.

LENGTH: 18–25".

VOICE: Series of low hoots, *hoo, hoo-hoo, hoo*.

RANGE:

HABITAT:
- woods
- parks
- suburbs

BARRED OWL
Strix varia

LOOK FOR: Dark eyes, bars on chest and neck, and a streaked belly. Black-ringed, gray face. **LENGTH:** 20".
VOICE: Loud *hoo-hoo-hoo*. **HABITAT:** Swampy forests.
RANGE: Southern Canada; eastern United States, Pacific Northwest.

BARN OWL
Tyto alba

LOOK FOR: Golden brown above and white below, a heart-shaped white facial disk, and dark eyes. **LENGTH:** 18". **VOICE:** Hisses, screeches, and clicks. **HABITAT:** Fields, forest edges, cities; also barns, attics, church steeples. **RANGE:** Widespread except northernmost regions.

93

EASTERN SCREECH-OWL
Otus asio

The Eastern Screech-Owl fearlessly defends the immediate area of its nest site and will strike at intruders. If they sense a threat during daylight, these owls freeze and depend on camouflage for protection.

Look for: A small red or gray owl with pale gray or orange facial disk ringed in black; large ear tufts and yellow eyes.

Length: 7–10".

Voice: Eerie, whistling wail that falls in pitch—heard mostly in spring and fall. Also gentle hoots and trills.

Range:

Habitat:
- forests
- wooded swamps
- cemeteries
- suburbs

SHORT-EARED OWL
Asio flammeus

Look for: Brown above and yellowish brown with brown stripes below. Black patches around yellow eyes. Tiny ear tufts. **Length:** 16". **Voice:** Long series of low *hoos*. Barks and squeals in breeding season. **Habitat:** Fields, grasslands, marshes. **Range:** Widespread.

BURROWING OWL
Speotyto cunicularia

Look for: A small, brown-and-white speckled owl that lives in burrows. Uses empty burrows of other animals or digs its own if needed. **Length:** 9". **Voice:** Soft *coo-coo*, and alarm chatter. **Habitat:** Open plains, fields, deserts. **Range:** Florida and western half of United States.

COMMON NIGHTHAWK
Chordeiles minor

Nighthawks are not hawks; they are members of the nightjar family. They do feed primarily during the evening and night hours, using their large mouths to catch hundreds of insects, such as flies and mosquitoes, in flight. They perch motionless in trees and on other structures during the day, with eyes tightly closed.

WHIP-POOR-WILL
Caprimulgus vociferus

LOOK FOR: A speckled-brown bird with white or yellowish-brown ring on throat. It is active at night, scratching for moths and other insects. It sleeps during the day, hidden by dead leaves. **LENGTH:** 9–10".
VOICE: Loudly repeats *whip-poor-will.*
HABITAT: Forest clearings. **RANGE:** East, Southwest; winter: Gulf Coast.

LOOK FOR: Hard to see when not in flight. Wide, white bar stands out on their long, pointed wings. Long, notched tail. The male has white throat and tail patches.

LENGTH: 8–10".

VOICE: Buzzy-sounding *beerb* or *peent.*

RANGE:

HABITAT:
- grasslands
- open woods
- cities

COMMON POORWILL
Phalaenoptilus nuttallii

LOOK FOR: Grayish brown with rounded tail and white band on throat. **LENGTH:** 7–8". **VOICE:** A gentle *poor-will.* **HABITAT:** Deserts, arid regions. Sometimes hibernates during cold spells. **RANGE:** Western United States; winter: Southwest.

97

RUBY-THROATED HUMMINGBIRD
Archilochus colubris

FEMALE

Hummingbirds have dazzling plumage and are incredibly skillful fliers. They can stop short in midair, hover like tiny helicopters, and only hummingbirds can fly backward. Their wings beat dozens of times a second, creating a low-pitched, bee-like buzzing. Their food is flower nectar and insects.

Look for: A long, needle-like, black bill. The male is shiny green above, with a white chest, green sides, and a ruby-red throat. The tail is black. The female and juveniles are similar but lack the red throat.

Length: 3½".

Voice: High, squeaky *chip*.

Range:

Habitat:
- woods
- fields
- gardens

ANNA'S HUMMINGBIRD
Calypte anna

Look for: Long, thin beak. Male: rose-colored crown and throat, with metallic green body. **Length:** 3–4". **Voice:** *Chip*. **Habitat:** Woods, gardens, thickets. **Range:** Pacific Coast to Arizona.

BROAD-TAILED HUMMINGBIRD
Selasphorus platycercus

Look for: Long beak. Male: green above, white below, rose-red throat. **Length:** 4". **Voice:** *Click*. **Habitat:** Mountain meadows, gardens, forests. **Range:** Western mountains.

RUFOUS HUMMINGBIRD
Selasphorus rufus

Look for: Male: red-brown with red throat. **Length:** 3–4". **Voice:** High, squealing *zeee*. **Habitat:** Forests, alpine meadows. **Range:** Pacific Northwest.

DOWNY WOODPECKER

Picoides pubescens

This small woodpecker is the one most often seen. It is frequently found in parks and gardens, and visits suet feeders in backyards. Like all woodpeckers, the Downy Woodpecker claims its territory by drumming—rapidly beating its bill against a hard surface. Each species has its own drumming sound and rhythm.

LOOK FOR: Sparrow-sized, with a short bill. It is black and white above, white below, with bold white spots on black wings. The male has a red patch at the back of the head.

LENGTH: 6–7".

VOICE: Calls with a soft *pik*. Also a descending whinny.

RANGE:

HABITAT:
- forests
- suburbs

NORTHERN FLICKER
Colaptes auratus

LOOK FOR: Brown with dark bars, pale belly with black spots. Eastern birds are yellow under wings, reddish in West. Male has black mustache (East) and red (West). **LENGTH:** 12–14". **VOICE:** Loud *wucka wucka*. **HABITAT:** Parks, open country. **RANGE:** Widespread.

PILEATED WOODPECKER
Dryocopus pileatus

LOOK FOR: A large bird with black-and-white stripes on red-crested head. **LENGTH:** 16–20". **VOICE:** Noisy *cuk-a, cuk-a, cuk-a.* **HABITAT:** Forests.

RANGE: Eastern half and northwestern region of North America.

YELLOW-BELLIED SAPSUCKER
Sphyrapicus varius

LOOK FOR: Red crown, pale yellow underparts. **LENGTH:** 8–9". **VOICE:** Nasal *cheeerrr.* **HABITAT:** Forests. **RANGE:** Canada, northeastern United States; mountains; winters: southern United States.

101

RED-BREASTED NUTHATCH

Sitta canadensis

The Red-breasted Nuthatch descends tree trunks head-first, searching for seeds and small insects. It is smaller than the White-breasted Nuthatch.

LOOK FOR: A small bird, blue-gray above, reddish below, with a bold white eyebrow stripe and a black line through the eye. It has a white face and chin and a black cap (in the female, cap is gray).

LENGTH: 4½".

VOICE: Nasal *nyank nyank.*

RANGE:

HABITAT:
- forests
- suburbs in winter and migration

WHITE-BREASTED NUTHATCH
Sitta carolinensis

LOOK FOR: Bluish-gray back, with a black cap, white below. Climbs down trees headfirst. **LENGTH:** 5–6". **VOICE:** Nasal *nyank nyank,* in spring, a rapid *to-what what what.* **HABITAT:** Forests, suburbs. **RANGE:** Widespread except southern plains.

BROWN CREEPER
Certhia americana

LOOK FOR: Streaked brown back, white below, thin curved bill. Creeps up tree trunks. **LENGTH:** 5". **VOICE:** High *ssst* or sweet, warbling song. **HABITAT:** Forests; parks and coastal areas during migration. **RANGE:** Widespread.

TREE SWALLOW
Tachycineta bicolor

Tree swallows nest in hollow trees, especially near water, but they also find and occupy backyard birdhouses. They compete vigorously with bluebirds who like the same size and type of house. During spring and summer evenings, tree swallows swoop and swirl through the air above lawns and trees, catching insects in their open mouths. They use white feathers both to line nests and for play.

LOOK FOR: The male is metallic blue-green above, white below. Female is duller. Juveniles are gray-brown above. The tail is notched.

LENGTH: 5–6".

VOICE: Calls *cheat-cheat*.

RANGE:

HABITAT:
- fields
- marshes
- waterways

BARN SWALLOW
Hirundo rustica

LOOK FOR: A small bird, steel-blue above, with long wings and deeply forked tail. **LENGTH:** 6–8". **VOICE:** Twitters, chatters. **HABITAT:** Farms (nests in barns), suburbs. **RANGE:** Widespread.

CHIMNEY SWIFT
Chaetura pelagica

LOOK FOR: A small, dark-gray bird with long wings and a short tail. **LENGTH:** 5". **VOICE:** Rapid chips and chitters. **HABITAT:** Nests in chimneys. **RANGE:** Eastern half of United States.

PURPLE MARTIN
Progne subis

LOOK FOR: Blue-black color. Gliding flight. **LENGTH:** 6–8½". **VOICE:** Chirps, trills. **HABITAT:** Farms, fields. **RANGE:** Widespread except Great Basin and western mountains.

105

WESTERN KINGBIRD
Tyrannus verticalis

The Western Kingbird, like all flycatchers, sits on tree stumps and other exposed perches waiting for the right moment to fly out and snap up a passing insect. It fiercely defends its nest and attacks much larger birds, if necessary.

LOOK FOR: Pale yellow belly and black tail edged with white on the sides. The crown and back are gray and there is a dark line through the eye.

LENGTH: 8–9".

VOICE: Shrill *kit* and *kit-kit-kiddle-dit.*

RANGE:

HABITAT:

- rivers
- grasslands
- farms
- deserts

EASTERN KINGBIRD
Tyrannus tyrannus

LOOK FOR: Blackish above, white below, white band at end of tail. **LENGTH:** 8–9".
VOICE: Sharp *dzee-dzee-dzee* and *kip-kipper.*
HABITAT: Forest edges, roadsides, farms.
RANGE: Widespread except Southwest.

GREAT-CRESTED FLYCATCHER
Myiarchus crinitus

LOOK FOR: Reddish tail and wings, yellow belly, slight crest. **LENGTH:** 7–9". **VOICE:** Loud *wheerup.* **HABITAT:** Forests, suburbs.
RANGE: East.

SCISSOR-TAILED FLYCATCHER
Tyrannus forficatus

LOOK FOR: Long, forked tail. Pale gray with pink sides and underwing. **LENGTH:** 14".
VOICE: Sharp *keet keet keet.* **HABITAT:** Open country. **RANGE:** Southern plains.

EASTERN PHOEBE
Sayornis phoebe

This tail-wagging bird arrives in the very early spring. It is the first species to have been banded in North America. It was an experiment conducted by John James Audubon, who in 1804 attached silver threads to the legs of young phoebes and found two that returned the following spring still wearing those threads.

LOOK FOR: A grayish-green flycatcher with a dark head; whitish underparts and throat. Lacks the eye ring and wing bars seen on similar species.

LENGTH: 6–7".

VOICE: Song: *fee-bee* repeated many times. Call: *chip.*

RANGE:

HABITAT:

- streamsides
- woods
- suburbs

LEAST FLYCATCHER
Empidonax minimus

LOOK FOR: Olive-brown back, yellowish white below, white eye ring. **LENGTH:** 4½–5". **VOICE:** Quick, repetitive *chebec, chebec*—like a cricket. **HABITAT:** Open woods, parks, suburbs. **RANGE:** Southern Canada, northern United States, Appalachian Mountains.

WESTERN WOOD-PEWEE
Contopus sordidulus

LOOK FOR: An olive-gray flycatcher with two wing bars. **LENGTH:** 6½". **VOICE:** Harsh *pheer-reet.* **HABITAT:** Open woods, orchards. **RANGE:** Western half of Canada and United States.

109

BLUE JAY
Cyanocitta cristata

The Blue Jay is a noisy, aggressive, and intelligent bird. Common and wide-ranging, the Blue Jay is admired for its beautiful plumage, but its reputation is clouded by its harsh treatment of other songbirds, chasing them from feeders and sometimes stealing their eggs and young.

LOOK FOR: This bird is blue above and grayish white below, with black markings on the face and tail. The tail has a white tip. Also, bright-blue crest, a black necklace, and black-and-white spots on the wings.

LENGTH: 11–12½".

VOICE: Noisy, harsh *jaay-jaay* or *tweedle tweedle*.

RANGE:

HABITAT:

- woods
- suburbs
- city parks

BELTED KINGFISHER
Ceryle alcyon

LOOK FOR: Blue-gray above and white below; bushy peaked crest, large bill.
LENGTH: 11–14". **VOICE:** Rattle. **HABITAT:** By rivers, lakes, coasts. **RANGE:** Widespread.

STELLER'S JAY
Cyanocitta stelleri

LOOK FOR: Large, black crest, bright blue body. **LENGTH:** 11–13". **VOICE:** Loud calls, cries, and screams. **HABITAT:** Forests. **RANGE:** Western regions.

WESTERN SCRUB-JAY
Aphelocoma californica

LOOK FOR: Blue head, tail, and wings with white belly. Has no crest. **LENGTH:** 11–13".
VOICE: Loud *jayy?* or *jree?*. **HABITAT:** Scrub and brush, open and desert country.
RANGE: Western regions.

111

AMERICAN CROW
Corvus brachyrhynchos

The American Crow is smart, bold, mischievous, noisy, and more numerous than ever. Crows will eat almost any food, and they use different calls to tell nearby crows about danger or food discoveries. Some crows (raised as pets) can imitate the human voice.

Look for: A glossy, black bird with squarish tail. Wings are rounded in flight with fingered wingtips.

Length: 17–21".

Voice: Loud *caw-caw*.

Range:

Habitat:

- woods
- farms
- shores
- roadsides
- urban areas

COMMON RAVEN
Corvus corax

Look for: A large, glossy, black bird with pointed wings in flight. Larger but shyer than the American Crow. **Length:** 21–27"
Voice: Low croak. **Habitat:** Forests, rocky coasts, western deserts. **Range:** Canada, western regions of United States, Appalachians.

BLACK-BILLED MAGPIE
Pica pica

Look for: A dramatic, black-and-white bird with green iridescent wings and long tail. **Length:** 17–22". **Voice:** High *maag maag maag*. **Habitat:** Open woods, prairies, farms. **Range:** Alaska, Great Plains to Pacific Northwest.

The worst winter weather does not bother the nimble chickadee as long as it has food to keep it warm beneath its fluffy, insulating feathers. The chickadee battles the cold by eating lots of seeds and berries, though its diet also includes insects and insect eggs. Young chickadees are as agile as their parents once out of the nest, just over two weeks after hatching.

LOOK FOR: Black cap and chin on a white cheek. Gray back, wings, and tail with buff-white below. Short black bill.

LENGTH: 4¾–5¾".

VOICE: Loud *chick-a-dee-dee* or *fee-bee*.

RANGE:

HABITAT:
- forests
- residential areas

TUFTED TITMOUSE
Parus bicolor

LOOK FOR: A gray-crested bird with reddish sides. **LENGTH:** 4½–6". **VOICE:** Whistles *peter peter peter*, repeated many times. **HABITAT:** Forests, swamps, parks, suburbs. **RANGE:** Eastern half of United States.

MOUNTAIN CHICKADEE
Parus gambeli

LOOK FOR: Resembles Black-capped Chickadee, but with thin, white line over eye and gray sides. **LENGTH:** 5½". **VOICE:** *Feebee feebee* and *chick-a-dee-dee-dee*. **HABITAT:** Evergreen trees in forests high up on mountains. **RANGE:** Western mountains.

115

HOUSE WREN
Troglodytes aedon

House Wrens are frequent visitors to backyards and gardens and are famous for taking advantage of unusual nesting places. They have been found nesting in tin cans, teapots, boots, shoes, and coat pockets. The House Wren constructs a messy collection of twigs and sticks and often builds more than one nest.

LOOK FOR: A brown bird, darker above than below, with wings and tail dotted or lightly barred black. This bird often holds its tail up.

LENGTH: 4½–5¼".

VOICE: Song: long, pleasing, gurgle. Call: *chuurr.*

RANGE: **HABITAT:**
- forest edges
- farms
- suburbs
- fields

MARSH WREN
Cistothorus palustris

LOOK FOR: A small wren, brown above with white and blackish streaks on back, white below. A white eyebrow.
LENGTH: 4–5". **VOICE:** Mechanical-sounding sputter, *tip-tip-tip-trrr.*
HABITAT: Marshes. **RANGE:** Widespread.

AMERICAN DIPPER
Cinclus mexicanus

LOOK FOR: A dark gray bird with short tail and yellow legs. Often dives into streams.
LENGTH: 7–8½".
VOICE: Loud, musical whistles. **HABITAT:** Mountain streams and high lakes. **RANGE:** Alaska and south through western mountains.

CAROLINA WREN
Thryothorus ludovicianus

LOOK FOR: This wren is reddish brown above, paler below, with a bold white eyebrow.
LENGTH: 4–5½". **VOICE:** Constant, cheery *tea kettle tea kettle.* **HABITAT:** Woods, suburbs.
RANGE: Eastern half of United States.

GOLDEN-CROWNED KINGLET
Regulus satrapa

The naturalist John K. Terres described the amazingly tiny kinglet as being "astonishingly fearless of people." It has "come into open cabins, allowed itself to be stroked at times and even picked up." An active bird, it flicks its wings constantly.

LOOK FOR: A very tiny, olive-green and yellowish bird with a bright yellow-orange crown marked with a black border (female's crown is yellow). Wings have yellowish edging and white wing bars. Short, notched tail.

LENGTH: 3½–4".

VOICE: Call: Three high *tsee* notes, followed by chatter.

RANGE:

HABITAT:
- conifer forests
- thickets

RUBY-CROWNED KINGLET
Regulus calendula

LOOK FOR: Greener than the Golden-crowned; no facial marks. Male: red crown tuft when excited. **LENGTH:** 3–4½". **VOICE:** Loud *tee tee, tew, tew.* **HABITAT:** Forests. **RANGE:** Widespread except central states.

BLUE-GRAY GNATCATCHER
Polioptila caerulea

LOOK FOR: Tiny bluish bird with long black tail, white eye ring. **LENGTH:** 4–5".
VOICE: Nasal *pzzz* or soft warble. **HABITAT:** Woods. **RANGE:** Widespread except Northwest and north-central states.

BUSHTIT
Psaltriparus minimus

LOOK FOR: A tiny, gray bird with a very long tail for its size. Some have a brown crown, others a gray crown. **LENGTH:** 3–4".
HABITAT: Forests. **RANGE:** Pacfic Northwest to Southwest.

119

Having lost their nesting tree holes to more aggressive European Starlings and House Sparrows, these gorgeous birds were decreasing in population. But thanks to bluebird fans who have built millions of special nest boxes, the sweet *chirrup* of these melodic songbirds once again fills the spring air.

LOOK FOR: The male is sky-blue above with an orange breast and throat, and a white belly. Female is duller.

LENGTH: 6–7½".

VOICE: Song: Soft warble. Call: musical *chur-lee.*

RANGE:

HABITAT:
- grasslands
- open forests
- yards
- farms

MOUNTAIN BLUEBIRD
Sialia currucoides

LOOK FOR: Male: sky-blue above, lighter below. Female: dull gray. **LENGTH:** 7". **VOICE:** Gentle warble. **HABITAT:** Meadows, grasslands. **RANGE:** Western regions.

INDIGO BUNTING
Passerina cyanea

LOOK FOR: Male: blue with darker wings and tail. Female: dull brown. **LENGTH:** 5½". **VOICE:** *Swee, swee, chew, chew.* **HABITAT:** Forest edges, roadsides. **RANGE:** East.

BLUE GROSBEAK
Guiraca caerulea

LOOK FOR: Male: dark blue with rust wing bars. Female: brown. **LENGTH:** 6–7". **VOICE:** Call: *clink.* **HABITAT:** Brushy fields. **RANGE:** Southern two-thirds of United States.

121

AMERICAN ROBIN
Turdus migratorius

Robins are often seen in spring and summer hopping along front lawns in search of earthworms. In fall and winter they turn to fruits and berries for their meals. Although originally a woodland species, they have thrived in modern suburbia.

LOOK FOR: A plump bird that is gray-brown above, rusty-orange below. The head and tail are black. The bill is yellow. The female's head and back are brown.

LENGTH: 9–11".

VOICE: Song: *cheerily, cheery-me*, rising and falling in pitch. Calls: *tut-tut-tut* and *tseep*.

RANGE:

HABITAT:
- woods
- farmlands
- gardens
- parks

EASTERN/SPOTTED TOWHEE
Pipilo erythrophthalmus/Pipilo maculatus

LOOK FOR: Spotted male (lives in West) is black above, white below, with reddish sides, white belly, and white spots on back. Eastern male lacks spots. (Previously this was one species, now split into two.) **LENGTH:** 7–8". **VOICE:** Eastern song is a cheery *drink-your-teee*. Spotted version sounds like *zeeee*.
HABITAT: Forest edges, brushy areas, parks. **RANGE:** Widespread.

HERMIT THRUSH
Catharus guttatus

LOOK FOR: A brown bird, smaller than a robin, with a reddish tail. Blurry dark spots on white belly. **LENGTH:** 6½–7½". **VOICE:** Flutelike notes or sharp *pit-pit-pit*. **HABITAT:** Forests, parks. **RANGE:** Widespread except central United States.

123

NORTHERN MOCKINGBIRD
Mimus polyglottos

The he Mockingbird is a tireless singer. Its Latin name means mimic of tongues, and it has an astonishing ability to repeat the songs of other birds as well as other sounds. Many reports of enormous repertories exist, the greatest being 39 bird songs and 50 calls—plus the sounds of a frog and a cricket.

LOOK FOR: A long-tailed songbird, gray above, paler below; wings have two slender wing bars and a large white patch. The outer tail feathers are white. Short, thin bill.

LENGTH: 9–11".

VOICE: Mimics other birds. Calls: loud *chack* and softer *chair*.

RANGE:

HABITAT:
- forest edges
- fields
- residential areas

GRAY CATBIRD
Dumetella carolinensis

LOOK FOR: A dark-gray songbird with black cap and long tail, with reddish color below tail. **LENGTH:** 8–9". **VOICE:** Catlike mew. Mimics other birds. **HABITAT:** Suburbs, parks. **RANGE:** Widespread.

BROWN THRASHER
Toxostoma rufum

LOOK FOR: Reddish-brown above, brown streaks on white below. **LENGTH:** 11½". **VOICE:** Musical phrases. **HABITAT:** Brushy fields, forest edges, gardens. **RANGE:** East.

LOGGERHEAD SHRIKE
Lanius ludovicianus

LOOK FOR: Gray above, white below, with black mask on face; white patches on black wings. **LENGTH:** 8–10". **VOICE:** Mixed sharp and sweet trills. **HABITAT:** Grasslands, open woods, parks. **RANGE:** Widespread.

125

RED-EYED VIREO
Vireo olivaceus

Like most songbirds, both male and female Red-eyed Vireos are good parents. They care for their young for 12 days before they are ready to leave their cup-shaped nest. Like other vireos, the Red-eyed is a tireless performer, singing all day—even when other birds are silenced by the midday heat.

Look for: A small, gray-capped, olive-green bird with a white eyebrow lined above with black. The eye is red, and a black line goes through it. The underparts are white; sides are yellowish. No wing bars.

Length: 5½–6½".

Voice: Song: a continuous *cher-eep cher-oop*, repeated up to 40 times a minute.

Range: **Habitat:**

- forests
- parks
- suburbs

WARBLING VIREO
Vireo gilvus

Look for: A small bird, gray-green above, white below, with a white eyebrow. **Length:** 5–6". **Voice:** Slow warble ending on high note. **Habitat:** Woods, shade trees, parks. **Range:** Widespread except Texas and Southeast.

SOLITARY VIREO
Vireo solitarius

Look for: A small bird with gray head, olive-green back, white below, with yellow sides and white eye rings. **Length:** 5–6". **Voice:** Series of musical phrases. **Habitat:** Forests. **Range:** Widespread except Plains; winter: Southeast.

127

YELLOW-RUMPED WARBLER
Dendroica coronata

EAST

The Myrtle Warbler, an eastern form, and Audubon's Warbler, a western form, are now considered the same species, the Yellow-rumped Warbler. Though they have different color markings, they interbreed freely.

Look for: In summer, the male is blue-gray above with black streaks on back. Yellow patches brighten the rump, crown, and sides. The throat is white in East, yellow in West. The female, winter male, and juveniles are brown with a yellow rump and white-spotted tail.

Length: 5–6".

Voice: Song: a slow trill. Call: a loud *check*.

Range:

Habitat:
- forests
- parks
- thickets
- residential areas

WILSON'S WARBLER
Wilsonia pusilla

Look for: Greenish above, golden yellow below, with black patch on crown. **Length:** 4½–5". **Voice:** Descending notes. **Habitat:** By streams, woods, bogs. **Range:** Canada, western mountains.

AMERICAN REDSTART
Setophaga ruticilla

Look for: Black above with bright orange patches, white below. **Length:** 4–5".
Voice: *Chewy-chewy-chewy.* **Habitat:** Forests.
Range: Widespread except Far West and Southwest.

BLACK-AND-WHITE WARBLER
Mniotilta varia

Look for: Black-and-white striped. Creeps down trees. **Length:** 4–5". **Voice:** *We see we see we see.* **Habitat:** Forests. **Range:** Eastern half of North America.

129

 # COMMON YELLOWTHROAT
Geothlypis trichas

The male yellowthroat has a continuous, energetic, and rhythmic song, singing while fluttering its wings, climbing, or jumping, and showing considerable excitement. The song varies from place to place, like regional dialects.

LOOK FOR: The male has a black face mask with a white line above it. The throat and chest are bright yellow. Upperparts are greenish brown. Female and juveniles lack the black mask.

LENGTH: 5–6".

VOICE: Song: loud, fast *witchity-witchity-witchity*.

RANGE:

HABITAT:

- wooded swamps
- grassy marshes

YELLOW WARBLER
Dendroica petechia

LOOK FOR: Yellow; some green on back. **LENGTH:** 4–5". **VOICE:** Cheery *sweet-sweet-sweet*. **HABITAT:** Thickets by streams and swamps. **RANGE:** Widespread.

NORTHERN PARULA
Parula americana

LOOK FOR: A blue warbler with a yellow throat and breast. **LENGTH:** 4". **VOICE:** Rising *zzzzz-zip*, dropping at end. **HABITAT:** Swampy woods. **RANGE:** East.

BLACK-THROATED BLUE WARBLER
Dendroica caerulescens

LOOK FOR: Grayish blue above, white below, with a black face and throat. **LENGTH:** 5". **VOICE:** Rising *zweer zweer zweer*. **HABITAT:** Forests. **RANGE:** Northeast, Great Lakes region.

131

NORTHERN CARDINAL
Cardinalis cardinalis

FEMALE

The cardinal derives its name from the red robes used by cardinals in the Roman Catholic Church. Cardinals have become increasingly common in northern areas, perhaps as a result of global warming. This adaptable bird breeds and winters in the same place.

LOOK FOR: The male is bright red with a black face, feathered red crest, and a cone-shaped red bill. The female has a pink bill and is grayish with dull red on crest, wings, and tail.

LENGTH: 8–9".

VOICE: Songs: whistled *wha-cheeer, wha-cheer;* a fast *weet-weet-weet.* Call: short *chip.*

RANGE:

HABITAT:
- woods
- shrubbery
- parks
- gardens

CEDAR WAXWING
Bombycilla cedrorum

LOOK FOR: Pointed crest, black face mask, and yellow band at end of gray tail. Also has red markings near wing tips. Travels in flocks. **LENGTH:** 6½–8". **VOICE:** High, lisping *ssee.* **HABITAT:** Forests, suburbs. **RANGE:** Widespread.

VERMILLION FLYCATCHER
Pyrocephalus rubinus

LOOK FOR: Male: brilliant red head and breast with brown wings, back, and tail. Female: Duller, with white and streaked underparts. **LENGTH:** 6". **VOICE:** *Pit, pit.* **HABITAT:** Streamsides, open country. **RANGE:** Southwest.

133

SONG SPARROW
Melospiza melodia

The Song Sparrow is the most common and widespread sparrow native to North America. The most northern Song Sparrows are larger and darker—quite different from the Song Sparrows we see in parks and on our lawns. Although Song Sparrows learn their music from other Song Sparrows, each bird creates its own variation. No two birds sing the same tune!

LOOK FOR: A brown sparrow streaked above with gray and black. Brown-black streaks on white underparts. Big, dark brown spot on chest. Moves tail up and down in flight.

LENGTH: 5–7".

VOICE: Song: *sweet sweet sweet towhee tritritritri.*

RANGE:

HABITAT:

- forests
- thickets
- marshes
- fields
- yards

DARK-EYED JUNCO
Junco hyemalis

LOOK FOR: A gray sparrow with a white belly and outer tail feathers, pink bill. **LENGTH:** 5–6½". **VOICE:** Soft, musical trill. **HABITAT:** Fields, forests, gardens. **RANGE:** Widespread.

HOUSE SPARROW
Passer domesticus

LOOK FOR: Black throat and breast; black, white, rust, and gray on head. **LENGTH:** 5–6". **VOICE:** Noisy chirruping. **HABITAT:** Cities, suburbs, farms. **RANGE:** Widespread.

WHITE-THROATED SPARROW
Zonotrichia albicollis

LOOK FOR: Brown-striped crown with yellow spot, white chin and breast. **LENGTH:** 6–7". **VOICE:** *Oh, sweet, Canada, Canada.* **HABITAT:** Forests. **RANGE:** Widespread.

135

The Eastern Meadowlark, well loved on the American prairie, has a cheerful song, among the first heard in spring. It constructs an elaborate covered nest on the ground. Like other grassland birds, meadowlarks are declining in number because their habitat is being taken over by humans.

LOOK FOR: Large black V on yellow breast. Upperparts are speckled with brown, black, and white. The gray bill is long and pointed.

LENGTH: 9–11".

VOICE: Song: whistles *tee-you-tee-yerr*. Call: harsh *sertt*.

RANGE:

HABITAT:
- grasslands
- prairies
- meadows
- farmlands

DICKCISSEL
Spiza americana

LOOK FOR: Yellow breast with black triangle on throat; rust-colored shoulder patch. **LENGTH:** 6". **VOICE:** *Dick-dick-dick-cissel.* **HABITAT:** Farms. **RANGE:** Great Lakes to Gulf Coast.

HORNED LARK
Eremophila alpestris

LOOK FOR: Bold stripes on face; black breast patch. Small "horns." **LENGTH:** 6–8". **VOICE:** Gentle *ti-ti.* **HABITAT:** Open country. **RANGE:** Widespread.

BOBOLINK
Dolichonyx oryzivorus

LOOK FOR: In summer, male is black with a white back and yellow on the back of the head. **LENGTH:** 6–8". **VOICE:** *Bob-o-link.* **HABITAT:** Prairies, meadows, marshes. **RANGE:** Oregon to eastern Canada.

137

BALTIMORE ORIOLE
Icterus galbula

The Baltimore Oriole was named after Lord Baltimore, the 17th-century Englishman who founded the Maryland colony and whose coat of arms was black and orange, like the bird. The Baltimore Orioles of baseball fame named their team after the bird. Now you know what the team colors are!

LOOK FOR: The male is black with bright orange on breast, rump, shoulder, and tail, and has one white bar on the wings. The female and juveniles are brownish above with dull yellow-orange below.

LENGTH: 7–8".

VOICE: Song: 4–8 piping whistles. Call: low, whistled *tee-tew*.

RANGE:

HABITAT:
- forest edges
- shade trees in cities and suburbs

BULLOCK'S ORIOLE
Icterus bullockii

LOOK FOR: Orange face, black eye line. Orange and black body and tail. **LENGTH:** 6–8". **VOICE:** Varied flutelike whistles. **HABITAT:** Shade trees, woods. **RANGE:** West.

SCARLET TANAGER
Piranga olivacea

LOOK FOR: Male: bright red with black wings and black tail. Female: olive-green. **LENGTH:** 6–7". **VOICE:** Warble like a robin's. **HABITAT:** Forests, parks. **RANGE:** Central and eastern United States.

WESTERN TANAGER
Piranga ludoviciana

LOOK FOR: Bright red head, yellow body, black wings and tail. **LENGTH:** 6–7". **VOICE:** Hoarse robin-like song. Call: *pit-er-ick*. **HABITAT:** Open forests. **RANGE:** Alaskan panhandle to Mexico.

RED-WINGED BLACKBIRD
Agelaius phoenicus

FEMALE

LOOK FOR: The male is glossy black with red shoulder patches bordered by yellow. The female and juveniles are brown with streaks.

LENGTH: 7–9½".

VOICE: Song: a musical *conk-a-ree*.

Calls: *check, tee-eek.*

RANGE:

HABITAT:

- marshes
- swamps
- fields

The Red-winged Blackbird is a marsh bird that has had a population explosion in recent years and can now be found nesting in fields, brushy places, and at woodland edges. They collect in enormous flocks in the fall, descending on cornfields like clouds of locusts.

COMMON GRACKLE
Quiscalus quiscula

LOOK FOR: Glossy black, blue, purple, and bronze. Long tail. Eyes are yellow. **LENGTH:** 12". **VOICE:** Harsh *tss-shkleet*. **HABITAT:** Woods, lawns. **RANGE:** East, Great Plains.

BROWN-HEADED COWBIRD
Molothrus ater

LOOK FOR: Male: black with a brown head and a cone-shaped bill. Female: gray. **LENGTH:** 6–8". **VOICE:** High and squeaky. **HABITAT:** Farms, open woods, suburbs. **RANGE:** Widespread.

EUROPEAN STARLING
Sturnus vulgaris

LOOK FOR: A short-tailed, blackish bird with glossy green and purple patches and a yellow bill. **LENGTH:** 7½–8½". **VOICE:** Harsh. Mimics others. **HABITAT:** Cities, farms. **RANGE:** Widespread.

141

HOUSE FINCH
Carpodacus mexicanus

The House Finch was introduced from the western United States to the East Coast by being freed from a cage on Long Island only fifty years ago. It has since become a common sight throughout the East. It is found in backyards and cities and will nest anywhere that is handy: in flowerpots, on buildings, or in other birds' nests.

LOOK FOR: The male is brown with orange to rosy-red on head, throat, breast, and rump. Heavy brown streaks mark the underparts. The female is brown but has no red.

LENGTH: 5–6".

VOICE: Canary-like warble ending with *jee* getting higher and higher in pitch.

RANGE: **HABITAT:**

- cities
- suburbs
- fields
- desert brush

PURPLE FINCH
Carpodacus purpureus

LOOK FOR: More raspberry-red than purple, with lighter underparts. Female and juveniles: brown and thickly striped. **LENGTH:** 5½–6½". **VOICE:** Rapid musical notes; *tik* in flight. **HABITAT:** Forests, suburbs. **RANGE:** Canada, Pacific Coast, Northeast.

PINE GROSBEAK
Pinicola enucleator

LOOK FOR: Mostly rosy-red with dark streaks on back, black tail, cone-shaped black bill, and two white bars on wings. Larger than the Purple Finch. **LENGTH:** 8–10". **VOICE:** Song: a musical warble. Call: a two- or three-note whistle. **HABITAT:** Forests. **RANGE:** Northern regions and western mountains.   143

AMERICAN GOLDFINCH
Carduelis tristis

Lined with soft milkweed fluff and thistledown, the nests of American Goldfinches are so thickly woven they can hold water. Because these birds eat the seeds of thistles and other plants, they usually settle near a good supply. Goldfinches nest late, in midsummer, when seeds begin to be plentiful.

LOOK FOR: In summer, the male is brilliant yellow with a black cap, notched tail, and bold white bars on black wings. The female is olive-green with a yellow throat and chest. In winter, males resemble females.

LENGTH: 5".

VOICE: Song: canary-like twittering. Calls: rising *sweee-eat* and *per chik-o-ree*.

RANGE:

HABITAT:
- fields
- forest edges
- grasslands
- suburbs

EVENING GROSBEAK
Coccothraustes vespertinus

LOOK FOR: Big, greenish-yellow, cone-shaped bill. Male: yellow and brown. Female: grayer than male. **LENGTH:** 7–8". **VOICE:** Short warbles. **HABITAT:** Forests, suburbs. **RANGE:** Widespread in winter except Southeast and Gulf states.

PINE SISKIN
Carduelis pinus

LOOK FOR: A brown-streaked finch with yellow patches. Flies in large flocks. **LENGTH:** 4½–5". **VOICE:** Buzzy, ascending *bzzzree*. **HABITAT:** Forests. **RANGE:** Widespread except Southeast and Gulf states. Breeds in northern states, West, Canada.

145

How to use the reference section

*Purple Finch
page 143*

The **Glossary** beginning on the opposite page contains terms used by ornithologists, naturalists, and birders. If you run across a word in this book that you don't understand, check the glossary for a definition. Also in this section is a listing of **Resources** including books, video tapes, audio tapes, CDs, Web sites, and organizations devoted to North American birds. Finally, there is an **Index** of all the species covered in the Field Guide section of this book.

The 50 state birds

Every state has an official state bird. All 50 state birds are listed and illustrated on the next five pages. The birds are shown in alphabetical order by state. If you live in Missouri, for example, go across the list, looking for states beginning with the letter M; the state bird for Missouri is the Eastern Bluebird. The common names in this list are those used by scientists and most birders. These names sometimes differ from those used by the states. For example, most birders call Alabama's state bird the Northern Flicker, but the state's official name for the bird is Yellowhammer.

Airfoil
A curved shape, like the wing of a bird or airplane, that allows lift in flight.

Alula
A small group of feathers at the bend of a bird's wing that helps produce extra lift in flight.

Barbs
Tiny branches that make up the vane of a feather.

Barbules
Tiny hooks that zip the barbs together.

Camouflage
Colors or patterns that help wild animals blend in with their environments.

Cap
The top of a bird's head.

Carotenoids
Pigments that give feathers red, yellow, or orange colors.

Chaparral
From the Spanish word for "scrub oak," a chaparral is a plant community of dense evergreen shrubs and small trees (2–8 feet high) most common on hillsides and mountains of California.

Conifers
Trees with needle-like leaves, such as pines and spruces.

Coverts
Rows of small feathers on the top and bottom of wings.

Crest
A tuft of feathers on the crown or back of a bird's head.

Crown
The top of a bird's head.

Deciduous
Leaf shedding. Trees that

Ruby-throated Hummingbird page 98

Alabama NORTHERN FLICKER 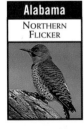	**Alaska** WILLOW PTARMIGAN 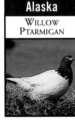	**Arizona** CACTUS WREN 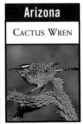	**Arkansas** NORTHERN MOCKINGBIRD 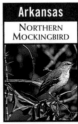	**California** CALIFORNIA QUAIL 
Colorado LARK BUNTING 	**Connecticut** AMERICAN ROBIN 	**Delaware** BLUE HEN CHICKEN 	**Florida** NORTHERN MOCKINGBIRD 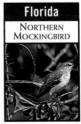	**Georgia** BROWN THRASHER 

shed their leaves in fall are called deciduous trees.

Ecosystem
All the plants and animals in an area, plus such non-living things as soil, air, and water needed by the living things to survive.

Embryo
An unborn animal.

Evolve
To change from generation to generation. Living things evolve through time; this is how new species develop.

Eye ring
A fleshy or feathered ring around the eye.

Field marks
Markings, colors, shapes, and other clues to a bird's identity.

Fledgling
A young bird that has just learned to fly and has left its nest. The process is called fledging.

Genus
A group of closely related species.

Habitat
The region where a particular species of plant or animal lives.

Yellow-headed Blackbird

Hawaii	Idaho	Illinois	Indiana	Iowa
HAWAIIAN GOOSE	MOUNTAIN BLUEBIRD	NORTHERN CARDINAL	NORTHERN CARDINAL	AMERICAN GOLDFINCH
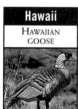	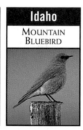	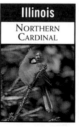	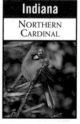	

Kansas	Kentucky	Louisiana	Maine	Maryland
WESTERN MEADOWLARK	NORTHERN CARDINAL	BROWN PELICAN	BLACK-CAPPED CHICKADEE	BALTIMORE ORIOLE
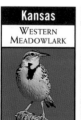		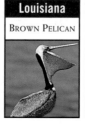		

Home Range (territory)
The area that a bird uses each day and defends against others of its species.

Incubate
To sit on eggs and keep them warm so that chicks will hatch.

Keratin
The flexible substance—similar to what your nails are made of—from which feathers, beaks, and claws are formed.

Lift
The raising force that allows birds to fly. It is provided by the air pressure underneath the wings, which is greater than the air pressure above the wings.

Lobe (lobate webbing)
A stiff flap that fringes each toe of a bird and allows it to swim faster. Grebes, phalaropes, and coots are the only North American birds with lobed feet. Most ducks and other waterfowl have webbed feet (toes connected by leathery skin).

Marshes
Treeless wetlands that develop around slow-moving bodies of water. Marshes have grasses, cattails, and sedges.

Melanins
Pigments that give feathers black, gray, or brown colors.

Migrate (migration)
To travel back and forth between two places when the seasons change.

Mimics
Birds that imitate the songs of other birds and animals.

Mixed forest
A forest in which trees with needle-like leaves (conifers) mix with trees that have broad leaves, such as maples and beeches.

Massachusetts	Michigan	Minnesota	Mississippi	Missouri
BLACK-CAPPED CHICKADEE	AMERICAN ROBIN	COMMON LOON	NORTHERN MOCKINGBIRD	EASTERN BLUEBIRD
			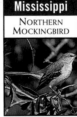	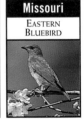

Montana	Nebraska	Nevada	New Hampshire	New Jersey
WESTERN MEADOWLARK	WESTERN MEADOWLARK	MOUNTAIN BLUEBIRD	PURPLE FINCH	AMERICAN GOLDFINCH
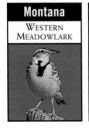	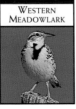	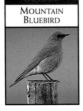		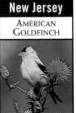

Molting
The shedding of old, worn-out feathers and the growing of new ones.

Mudflats
Muddy areas once covered by water but now exposed.

Nape
The back of a bird's head.

Navigation
The use of points, such as stars, to help determine where you are and to direct you to your destination.

Pesticides
Chemicals that are used to kill insects and other pests.

Plumage
A bird's coat of feathers.

Precocial
Maturing early. Precocial baby birds are able to see, move, and feed themselves as soon as they hatch.

Preening
The grooming and cleaning of feathers.

Primaries
Long flight feathers near the tip of a wing.

Range
The geographic area normally inhabited by a species.

Secondaries
Shortest flight feathers of a wing. They are closer to the body than primaries.

Scrub oak
A small tree that forms low thickets. Western scrub oaks are sometimes evergreen.

Shaft
The stiff quill that runs down the middle of a feather.

Species
A group of closely related living things, such as birds, that usually mate with one another.

New Mexico	New York	North Carolina	North Dakota	Ohio
GREATER ROADRUNNER	EASTERN BLUEBIRD	NORTHERN CARDINAL	WESTERN MEADOWLARK	NORTHERN CARDINAL

Oklahoma	Oregon	Pennsylvania	Rhode Island	South Carolina
SCISSOR-TAILED FLYCATCHER	WESTERN MEADOWLARK	RUFFED GROUSE	RHODE ISLAND RED CHICKEN	CAROLINA WREN

GLOSSARY AND THE 50 STATE BIRDS

Syrinx
The "voice box" in a bird's throat that produces songs.

Talons
Sharp curved claws of hawks, owls, and other hunting birds.

Taxonomy
The classification of plants and animals based on their relationship to one another.

Tundra
A treeless plain like that extending from the northern coast of Canada south to Canada's evergreen forests. Tundras have a constant frozen layer beneath the surface of the ground.

Vane
The soft sheets on either side of a feather's central shaft.

Wetlands
Marshes, swamps, bogs, or any land with a lot of water in the soil.

Wing bar
A bar of contrasting color on the small wing feathers.

Yolk
The yellow globe inside an egg that provides food for the growing embryo.

*House Wren
page 116*

South Dakota	Tennessee	Texas	Utah	Vermont
RING-NECKED PHEASANT	NORTHERN MOCKINGBIRD	NORTHERN MOCKINGBIRD	CALIFORNIA GULL	HERMIT THRUSH
	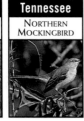	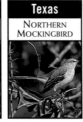		

Virginia	Washington	West Virginia	Wisconsin	Wyoming
NORTHERN CARDINAL	AMERICAN GOLDFINCH	NORTHERN CARDINAL	AMERICAN ROBIN	WESTERN MEADOWLARK

FOR FURTHER READING

About Birds: A Guide for Children
John Sill (Illustrator) and
Cathryn P. Sill
Peachtree Publishers, 1991

Orchard Oriole

Amazing Birds
(Eyewitness Juniors Series)
Alexandra Parsons
Alfred A. Knopf, 1990

Amazing Birds of Prey
(Eyewitness Juniors Series)
Alexandra Parsons
Alfred A. Knopf, 1992

Audubon's Birds of America
John James Audubon
Thunder Bay Press, 1994

The Audubon Society Encyclopedia of North American Birds
John K. Terres
Wings Books, 1995

The Big Golden Book of Backyard Birds
Kathleen Daly
Golden Books, 1990

Bird Life: A Guide to the Behavior and Biology of Birds
(Golden Guide Series)
Golden Books, 1991

Bird Study
Boy Scouts of America, 1984

Bird Wise
P. M. Hickman
New England Press, 1988

Birds and How They Live
David Burnie
Dorling Kindersley, 1992

Book of North American Birds
Reader's Digest, 1993

Everybody's Everywhere Backyard Bird Book
Editors of Klutz Press
Klutz Press, 1992

Eyewitness Books: Birds
David Burnie
Alfred A. Knopf, 1988

Eyewitness Books: Eagle and Birds of Prey
Eyewitness Books Staff
Alfred A. Knopf, 1997

The Great Bird Detective
David Elcome
Chronicle, 1995

Macmillan Field Guides Birds of North America (Eastern Region)
John Bull, Edith Bull, Gerald Gold, Peter D. Prall
Collier Books, 1985

Mysteries and Marvels of Bird Life
I. Wallace, R. Hume, R. Morris
Usborne Publishing Ltd., 1984

National Audubon Society Field Guide to North American Birds (Eastern Region)
John Bull and John Farrand, Jr.
Alfred A. Knopf, 1995

National Audubon Society Field Guide to North American Birds (Western Region)
Miklos D. F. Udvardy and
John Farrand, Jr.
Alfred A. Knopf, 1995

National Audubon Society Pocket Guide to Familiar Birds of Lakes and Rivers
Richard K. Walton
Alfred A. Knopf, 1994

National Audubon Society Pocket Guide to Familiar Birds of North America (Eastern Region)
Alfred A. Knopf, 1986

National Audubon Society Pocket Guide to Familiar Birds of North America (Western Region)
Alfred A. Knopf, 1986

National Audubon Society Pocket Guide to Songbirds and Familiar Backyard Birds (Eastern Region)
Wayne R. Petersen
Alfred A. Knopf, 1994

National Audubon Society Pocket Guide to Songbirds and Familiar Backyard Birds (Western Region)
Richard K. Walton
Alfred A. Knopf, 1994

Peterson First Guides: Birds
Roger Tory Peterson
Houghton Mifflin, 1986

Project Puffin: How We Brought Puffins Back to Egg Rock
Stephen W. Kress, as told by
Pete Salmansohn
Tilbury House, 1997

TAPES AND DISKS

Audubon Society's Video Guide to Birds of North America, Volumes I-V (Videocassettes)
Godfrey Studio Productions

Backyard Bird Song (Audiotape)
Roger Tory Peterson (editor)
Peterson's Field Guides
Houghton Mifflin, 1991

Birding by Ear (Eastern)
(Audiotape)
Roger Tory Peterson (editor)
Peterson Field Guides
Houghton Mifflin, 1989

Birding by Ear (Central and Western) (Audiotape)
Roger Tory Peterson (editor)
Peterson Field Guides
Houghton Mifflin, 1990

Eyewitness: BIRD (CD)
Dorling Kindersley Ltd. and BBC
Lionheart Television
International, Inc., 1994

National Audubon Society Guide to North American Birds
(Interactive CD-ROM)
Knopf Publishing Group, 1996

Paul Parkranger and the Mystery of the Disappearing Ducks (Wetlands)
(Interactive Laser Videodisk)
MCI/Coronet
(Simon & Schuster, Inc.)

ORGANIZATIONS

American Birding Association
P.O. Box 6599
Colorado Springs, CO 80934

Hawk Mountain Sanctuary Association
1700 Hawk Mountain Road
Kempton, PA 19529-9449
Tel: 610-756-6961

Hawk Watch International
P.O. Box 660
Salt Lake City, UT 84110-0660
Tel: 801-524-8511
E-mail:
hawkwatch@charitiesusa.com

National Audubon Society
700 Broadway
New York, NY 10003-9562
Tel: 212-979-3000
1-800-274-4201
E-mail: tcanela@audubon.org

National Wildlife Federation
8925 Leesburg Pike
Vienna, VA 22184
Tel: 703-790-4100

The Nature Conservancy
International Headquarters
1815 North Lynn Street
Arlington, VA 22209
Tel: 703-841-5300

The Peregrine Fund
566 West Flying Hawk Lane
Boise, ID 83709
Tel: 208-362-3716
E-mail: tpf@peregrinefund.org

Sierra Club
85 Second Street, Second Floor
San Francisco, CA 94105-3441
Tel: 415-977-5500

WEB SITES

Audubon Web site:
www.audubon.org

Audubon Web site for Kids:
www.audubon.org/kid/index.html

Backyard Birding:
www.bcpl.lib.md.us/~tross/by/backyard.html

Birding on the Web:
www.birder.com

Birding with the Birdman:
members.aol.com/danbirdman/birdman.htm

Birdlinks:
www.phys.rug.nl/mk/people/wpv/birdlink.html

National Museum of Natural History Smithsonian Institution, Division of Birds:
www.nmnh.si.edu/vert/birds

Peterson Online:
www.petersononline.com

Selected Links to Other Ornithological Sites:
www.nmnh.edu/vert/birds/brdsites.html

Stanton Bird Club:
www.avcnet.org/stanton

Yahoo Web site:
www.yahoo.com/Recreation/Outdoors/Birding

Cedar Waxwing page 133

INDEX

*Great Blue Heron
page 46*

INDEX

Tundra Swan page 57

*Barn Swallow
page 105*

PHOTO/ILLUSTRATION CREDITS

89b: Nell Bolen/Photo Researchers
89c: Chuck Gordon
90: Arthur Morris/Birds As Art
91a: Arthur Morris/Birds As Art
91b: Tim Zurowski
91c: Larry Ditto
92: E. R. Degginger/Color-Pic, Inc.
93a: Gay Bumgarner
93b: John Serrao
94: Ron Austing
95a: Jim Roetzel
95b: Sharon Cummings
96: Arthur Morris/Birds As Art
97a: Ron Austing
97b: C. Allan Morgan
98a (male): Ron Austing
98b (female inset): Nick Bergkessel/Photo
  Researchers
99a: G.C. Kelley/Photo Researchers
99b: G.C. Kelley
99c: Tim Zurowski
100: E. R. Degginger/Color-Pic, Inc.
101a: Tom Vezo
101b: Ron Austing
101c: Gregory K. Scott/Photo
  Researchers
102: Rob Curtis/The Early Birder
103a: Tom Vezo
103b: Rob Curtis/The Early Birder
104: Tim Zurowski
105a: Tim Zurowski
105b: Ron Austing
105c: Rob Curtis/The Early Birder
106: Brian E. Small
107a: Bates Littlehales
107b: M.H. Sharp/Photo Researchers
107c: Rob Curtis/The Early Birder
108: Kevin T. Karlson
109a: Brian E. Small
109b: Herbert Clarke
110: Jim Roetzel
111a: Steve Bentsen
111b: Brian E. Small
111c: Brian E. Small
112: Simpson & Co. Nature Stock
113a: Gerald & Buff Corsi/Focus on
  Nature, Inc.
113b: C. Allan Morgan
114: Tom Vezo
115a: L. West/Photo Researchers
115b: Brian E. Small
116: Harold Lindstrom
117a: Tom Vezo
117b: Anthony Mercieca/Photo
  Researchers
117c: Tom Ulrich
118: Rob Curtis/The Early Birder
119a: Ron Austing
119b: Brian E. Small
119c: Tim Zurowski
120: Stephen G. Maka
121a: Larry Ditto
121b: Brian E. Small
121c: Kevin T. Karlson
122: Tom Vezo
123a: Tim Zurowski
123b: Rob Curtis/The Early Birder
124: Tom Vezo
125a: Brian E. Small
125b: James H. Robinson
125c: Steve & Dave Maslowski/Photo
  Researchers

126: Ron Austing
127a: Herbert Clarke
127b: Kathy Lindstrom
128a (Audubon's): Brian E. Small
128b (Myrtle): Ron Austing
129a: Brian E. Small
129b: Brian E. Small
129c: Brian E. Small
130: Herbert Clarke
131a: Brian E. Small
131b: Brian E. Small
131c: Brian E. Small
132a: Jim Roetzel
132b (female inset): Jim Roetzel
133a: Jeffrey Rich
133b: C.K. Lorenz/Photo Researchers
134: Rob Curtis/The Early Birder
135a: Gay Bumgarner
135b: Harold Lindstrom
135c: Tom Vezo
136: Ron Austing
137a: Steve & Dave Maslowski/Photo
  Researchers
137b: Mark Wallner
137c: Steve & Dave Maslowski/Photo
  Researchers
138: Simpson & Co. Nature Stock
139a: Betty Randall
139b: Jim Roetzel
139c: Brian E. Small
140a: Sharon Cummings
140b (female inset): Stephen J.
  Krasemann/Photo Researchers
141a: Tom Ulrich
141b: Harry M. Walker
141c: Harold Hoffman/Photo Researchers
142: Tom Vezo
143a: Tim Zurowski
143b: Stephen J. Krasemann/Photo
  Researchers
144: Gregory K. Scott/Photo Researchers
145a: Stephen J. Krasemann/Photo
  Researchers
145b: Brian E. Small
146: Tim Zurowski
147a (hummingbird): Nick Bergkessel/
  Photo Researchers
147 (Alabama): Tom Vezo
147 (Alaska): François Gohier/Photo
  Researchers
147 (Arizona): G.C. Kelley/Photo
  Researchers
147 (Arkansas): Tom Vezo
147 (California): Hugh P. Smith
147 (Colorado): Rod Planck/Photo
  Researchers
147 (Connecticut): Tom Vezo
147 (Delaware): Delaware Tourism Office
147 (Florida): Tom Vezo
147 (Georgia): James Robinson
148a (blackbird): Rod Planck/Photo
  Researchers
148 (Hawaii): Stephen J. Krasemann/
  Photo Researchers
148 (Idaho): Frank Oberle
148 (Illinois): Jim Roetzel
148 (Indiana): Jim Roetzel
148 (Iowa): Gregory K. Scott/Photo
  Researchers
148 (Kansas): Rod Planck/Photo
  Researchers
148 (Kentucky): Jim Roetzel

148 (Louisiana): Tom Vezo
148 (Maine): Tom Vezo
148 (Maryland): Simpson & Co. Nature
  Stock
149 (Massachussets): Tom Vezo
149 (Michigan): Tom Vezo
149 (Minnesota): Harold Lindstrom
149 (Mississippi): Tom Vezo
149 (Missouri): Stephen G. Maka
149 (Montana): Rod Planck/Photo
  Researchers
149 (Nebraska): Rod Planck/Photo
  Researchers
149 (Nevada): Frank Oberle
149 (New Hampshire): Tim Zurowski
149 (New Jersey): Gregory K. Scott/
  Photo Researchers
150 (New Mexico): Chuck Gordon
150 (New York): Stephen G. Maka
150 (North Carolina): Jim Roetzel
150 (North Dakota): Rod Planck/Photo
  Researchers
150 (Ohio): Jim Roetzel
150 (Oklahoma): Rob Curtis/The Early
  Birder
150 (Oregon): Rod Planck/Photo
  Researchers
150 (Pennsylvania): Tom Vezo
150 (Rhode Island): Rod Planck/Photo
  Researchers
150 (South Carolina): Tom Ulrich
151a (wren): Harold Lindstrom
151 (South Dakota): Tom Vezo
151 (Tennessee): Tom Vezo
151 (Texas): Tom Vezo
151 (Utah): Leonard Lee Rue III/Photo
  Researchers
151 (Vermont): Rob Curtis/The Early
  Birder
151 (Virginia): Jim Roetzel
151 (Washington): Gregory K. Scott/
  Photo Researchers
151 (West Virginia): Jim Roetzel
151 (Wisconsin): Tom Vezo
151 (Wyoming): Rod Planck/Photo
  Researchers
152: E. R. Degginger/Color-Pic, Inc.
153: Wayne Lankinen
154: Jeff Lepore/Photo Researchers
155: Jim Roetzel
156: Jeff Lepore/Photo Researchers
157: Anthony Mercieca/Photo
  Researchers
Front Cover: Gregory K. Scott/Photo

*Photo Researchers:
Photo Researchers, Inc.
60 East 56th Street
New York, NY 10022

Prepared and produced by
Chanticleer Press, Inc., and Chic Simple Design

Founder, Chanticleer Press, Inc.: Paul Steiner

Publisher, Chanticleer Press, Inc.: Andrew Stewart
Publishers, Chic Simple Design: Jeff Stone, Kim Johnson Gross

Chanticleer Staff:
Editor-in-Chief: Amy K. Hughes
Director of Production: Alicia Mills
Production Associate: Philip Pfeifer
Photo Editor: Zan Carter
Senior Editor: Lauren Weidenman
Managing Editors: Kristina Lucenko and Edie Locke
Editorial Assistant: Karin Murphy

Project Editors: Edward S. Barnard, Sharon Fass Yates
Bookmark Associates, Inc.

Chic Simple Design Staff:
Art Direction/Design: Takuyo Takahashi
Production/Design: Jinger Peissig
Project Coordinator: Gillian Oppenheim
Production: Camilla Marstrand
Design Interns: Kathryn Hammill, Danielle Huthart,
Diane Shaw, Sylvie Pusztaszeri

Writer (The world of birds, How to look at birds): Scott Weidensaul
Consultant: Robert E. Budlinger
Copy Editors: Kristina Bohl, Sarah Burns
Illustrator: Taina Litwak
Icon Illustrator: Holly Kowitt
Studio Photographer: David Bashaw

Scholastic Inc. Staff:
Editorial Director: Wendy Barish, Creative Director: David Saylor,
Managing Editor: Manuela Soares, Production Editor: Sean Gallagher,
Manufacturing Manager: Janet Castiglione

Original Series Design: Chic Simple Design, Takuyo Takahashi